READINGS ON

HAMLET

OTHER TITLES IN THE GREENHAVEN PRESS LITERARY COMPANION SERIES:

AMERICAN AUTHORS

Maya Angelou
Stephen Crane
Emily Dickinson
William Faulkner
F. Scott Fitzgerald
Nathaniel Hawthorne
Ernest Hemingway
Herman Melville
Arthur Miller
Eugene O'Neill
Edgar Allan Poe
John Steinbeck
Mark Twain
Thornton Wilder

AMERICAN LITERATURE

The Adventures of
  Huckleberry Finn
The Adventures of Tom
  Sawyer
The Catcher in the Rye
The Crucible
Death of a Salesman
The Glass Menagerie
The Grapes of Wrath
The Great Gatsby
Of Mice and Men
The Old Man and the Sea
The Pearl
The Scarlet Letter
A Separate Peace

BRITISH AUTHORS

Jane Austen
Joseph Conrad
Charles Dickens

BRITISH LITERATURE

Animal Farm
The Canterbury Tales
Great Expectations
Julius Caesar
Lord of the Flies
Macbeth
Pride and Prejudice
Romeo and Juliet
Shakespeare: The Comedies
Shakespeare: The Histories
Shakespeare: The Sonnets
Shakespeare: The Tragedies
A Tale of Two Cities
Wuthering Heights

WORLD AUTHORS

Fyodor Dostoyevsky
Homer
Sophocles

WORLD LITERATURE

All Quiet on the Western
  Front
The Diary of a Young Girl
A Doll's House

THE GREENHAVEN PRESS
Literary Companion
TO BRITISH LITERATURE

READINGS ON

HAMLET

Don Nardo, *Book Editor*

David L. Bender, *Publisher*
Bruno Leone, *Executive Editor*
Bonnie Szumski, *Series Editor*

Greenhaven Press, Inc., San Diego, CA

Every effort has been made to trace the owners of copyrighted material. The articles in this volume may have been edited for content, length, and/or reading level. The titles have been changed to enhance the editorial purpose. Those interested in locating the original source will find the complete citation on the first page of each article.

Library of Congress Cataloging-in-Publication Data

Readings on Hamlet / Don Nardo, book editor.
      p.   cm. — (The Greenhaven Press literary
companion to British literature)
    Includes bibliographical references (p.   ) and index.
   ISBN 1-56510-837-X (lib. : alk. paper). —
ISBN 1-56510-836-1 (pbk. : alk. paper)
    1. Shakespeare, William, 1564–1616. Hamlet.
I. Nardo, Don, 1947–   . II. Title: Hamlet. III. Series.
PR2807.R4   1999
822.3'3—dc21   98-29856
                                             CIP

Cover photo: AKG, London

Copyright ©1999 by Greenhaven Press, Inc.
PO Box 289009
San Diego, CA 92198-9009
Printed in the U.S.A.

66 What a piece of work is a man! how noble in reason! how infinite in faculties! in form and moving how express and admirable! in action how like an angel! in apprehension how like a god! the beauty of the world, the paragon of animals! And yet to me what is this quintessence of dust? 99

—Hamlet
Act 2, scene 2

CONTENTS

Chapter 1: The Plot, Structure, Setting, and Wordplay of *Hamlet*

The story of young Prince Hamlet, who meets the ghost of his recently deceased father, learns that the king was murdered, and swears revenge, is one of the most familiar in world literature. A renowned expert on Shakespeare's plays tells how Hamlet, after much indecision and delay, gets his revenge but in the process meets his own untimely end.

The ghost on the battlements who urges Hamlet to seek revenge and Hamlet's pretended madness are but two of the standard elements that Elizabethan playwrights incorporated into their popular revenge plays. But though Shakespeare followed the accepted formula, he also transcended it, making the title character a plaintive voice that comments profoundly on the human condition and meaning of life.

The stately Danish royal court at Elsinore Castle is *Hamlet*'s setting. On the surface, all seems pleasant and calm. But traditional courtly speech and manners only hide the lust, greed, and brutality that lurk in the shadows, corrupt realities that the title character relentlessly attempts to expose.

During the course of the play, Hamlet stops several times and talks to himself aloud, exposing to the audience his innermost thoughts and feelings, as well as his plans for getting revenge on his uncle. Through these soliloquies and other devices, Shakespeare created a special and crucial connection between the main character and the audience.

Chapter 2: The Play's Pivotal Characters

intrigues and double-dealing of the royal court. Like Hamlet, Claudius, and other important male figures in that court, therefore, Laertes, despite his many good qualities, has a darker side that contributes to his eventual downfall.

Chapter 3: Themes and Ideas Developed in *Hamlet*

certain circumstances, an honorable alternative. For a Christian like Hamlet, however, suicide is a sin. And taking revenge on his uncle might anger God and bring on eternal damnation. In these and other ways, Hamlet's Christian beliefs cause him to doubt, to hesitate, and ultimately to act less decisively than a pagan hero might.

Chapter 4: Diverse Ways of Interpreting and Staging *Hamlet*

FOREWORD

*"'Tis the good reader that
makes the good book."*

Ralph Waldo Emerson

The story's bare facts are simple: The captain, an old and scarred seafarer, walks with a peg leg made of whale ivory. He relentlessly drives his crew to hunt the world's oceans for the great white whale that crippled him. After a long search, the ship encounters the whale and a fierce battle ensues. Finally the captain drives his harpoon into the whale, but the harpoon line catches the captain about the neck and drags him to his death.

A simple story, a straightforward plot—yet, since the 1851 publication of Herman Melville's *Moby-Dick*, readers and critics have found many meanings in the struggle between Captain Ahab and the whale. To some, the novel is a cautionary tale that depicts how Ahab's obsession with revenge leads to his insanity and death. Others believe that the whale represents the unknowable secrets of the universe and that Ahab is a tragic hero who dares to challenge fate by attempting to discover this knowledge. Perhaps Melville intended Ahab as a criticism of Americans' tendency to become involved in well-intentioned but irrational causes. Or did Melville model Ahab after himself, letting his fictional character express his anger at what he perceived as a cruel and distant god?

Although literary critics disagree over the meaning of *Moby-Dick*, readers do not need to choose one particular interpretation in order to gain an understanding of Melville's novel. Instead, by examining various analyses, they can gain numerous insights into the issues that lie under the surface of the basic plot. Studying the writings of literary critics can also aid readers in making their own assessments of *Moby-Dick* and other literary works and in developing analytical thinking skills.

The Greenhaven Literary Companion Series was created with these goals in mind. Designed for young adults, this unique anthology series provides an engaging and comprehensive introduction to literary analysis and criticism. The essays included in the Literary Companion Series are chosen for their accessibility to a young adult audience and are expertly edited in consideration of both the reading and comprehension levels of this audience. In addition, each essay is introduced by a concise summation that presents the contributing writer's main themes and insights. Every anthology in the Literary Companion Series contains a varied selection of critical essays that cover a wide time span and express diverse views. Wherever possible, primary sources are represented through excerpts from authors' notebooks, letters, and journals and through contemporary criticism.

Each title in the Literary Companion Series pays careful consideration to the historical context of the particular author or literary work. In-depth biographies and detailed chronologies reveal important aspects of authors' lives and emphasize the historical events and social milieu that influenced their writings. To facilitate further research, every anthology includes primary and secondary source bibliographies of articles and/or books selected for their suitability for young adults. These engaging features make the Greenhaven Literary Companion series ideal for introducing students to literary analysis in the classroom or as a library resource for young adults researching the world's great authors and literature.

Exceptional in its focus on young adults, the Greenhaven Literary Companion Series strives to present literary criticism in a compelling and accessible format. Every title in the series is intended to spark readers' interest in leading American and world authors, to help them broaden their understanding of literature, and to encourage them to formulate their own analyses of the literary works that they read. It is the editors' hope that young adult readers will find these anthologies to be true companions in their study of literature.

INTRODUCTION

What if all the plays ever written disappeared, except for William Shakespeare's *Hamlet*, which somehow miraculously survived? This was the thought-provoking question asked by the great early-twentieth-century Russian stage director Vsevolod Meyerhold. His answer: "All the theaters in the world would be saved. They could all put on *Hamlet* and be successful."[1] Did Meyerhold exaggerate? Yes. But most who love literature and the theater would say "only a little." Indeed, *Hamlet* is often referred to as the greatest play ever written by the greatest playwright who ever lived. And even if this statement, too, is exaggerated, the play's unmatched record of performances and veritable avalanche of literary and artistic interpretations demonstrate that it is surely the most popular play ever written.

Since it was first staged in London in about 1601, *Hamlet* has been the world's most often performed play. It has attracted the greatest actors of each succeeding generation, all drawn by the beauty and emotional power of the lines and the challenge of discovering what makes the complex title character tick. "You can play it and play it as many times as opportunity occurs," stated renowned actor Laurence Olivier, "and still not get to the bottom of its box of wonders. . . . Once you have played it, it will devour you and obsess you for the rest of your life."[2] A more recent stage Hamlet, Stephen Berkoff, more concisely quipped, "In every actor is a Hamlet struggling to get out."[3]

In addition to its tens of thousands of stage presentations over the years, *Hamlet* has been filmed nearly fifty times, with stars ranging from Laurence Olivier to Mel Gibson in the title role. A testimonial to the play's universality is that among these movies are a number made in Italy, India, the African nation of Ghana, and other foreign cultures seemingly far removed from the story's original setting of medieval Denmark. *Hamlet* has also inspired twenty-six ballets, six operas, and dozens of other musical works. And it is the most quoted, written about, and studied play in the world, with hundreds of new books, articles, and reviews appearing every year.

What makes *Hamlet* so appealing to so many different people is undoubtedly its deep exploration of some of the basic truths of the human experience. Through the play's characters and actions, scholars Phyllis Abrahms and Alan Brody point out, "Shakespeare probes the nature of death, of fate, of madness. He reveals the eternal conflicts between reality and illusion, faith and despair, the mind and the body."[4] Because each succeeding generation contemplates anew these essential human themes and values, each invariably searches *Hamlet* for some fresh insight or new twist on an old idea. And for these reasons, the play will no doubt remain as important and popular to future generations as it is today.

The essays selected for Greenhaven's *Readings on* Hamlet provide teachers and students with a wide range of information and opinion about the play and its author's style, themes, and outlook on the human condition. All of the authors cited in this compilation are or were (until their deaths) noted professors at leading colleges and universities, scholars specializing in Shakespearean studies, or famous Shakespearean actors. Each of the essays in this literary companion explains or discusses in detail a specific, narrowly focused topic. The introduction to each essay previews the main points, and inserts interspersed within the essays serve as examples of ideas expressed by the authors, offer supplementary information, and add authenticity and color. These inserts come from *Hamlet* or other plays by Shakespeare, from critical commentary about these works, or from other scholarly sources.

Above all, this literary companion is designed to enhance the reader's understanding and enjoyment of the most famous play in literature, a work that remains an endless source of theatrical and literary fascination. As noted drama professor Marvin Rosenberg puts it:

> We will all keep on learning new things about *Hamlet* as long as people love poetry and drama. Like the actors who wish they could play it forever, I could go on reading and writing about the play at least as long, and learn new things every day. Again—*Hamlet* is bottomless.[5]

NOTES

1. Quoted in Dmitri Shostakovich, *Testimony: The Memoirs of Dmitri Shostakovich*. Trans. Antonina W. Bouis. London: Faber, 1981, p. 84.

2. Laurence Olivier, *On Acting.* New York: Simon and Schuster, 1986, pp. 76–77.

3. Quoted in Norrie Epstein, *The Friendly Shakespeare: A Thoroughly Painless Guide to the Best of the Bard.* New York: Viking Penguin, 1993, p. 336.

4. Phyllis Abrahms and Alan Brody, introduction to *Hamlet,* ed. Michael Martin. New York: Prestige Books, 1968, pp. xviii–xix.

5. Marvin Rosenberg, *The Masks of Hamlet.* Newark: University of Delaware Press, 1992, p. xvi.

WILLIAM SHAKESPEARE: A BIOGRAPHY

Somewhere in the world today, as has happened hundreds of thousands of times before and will happen countless times hereafter, a curtain is rising on a new performance of William Shakespeare's *Hamlet*. Some of those in the audience have seen the play before, but many are attending for the first time. Regardless of the quality of the production, after the curtain falls audiences new to *Hamlet* will invariably leave stamped with an indelible memory, one that will color, by way of comparison, any and all live or filmed productions of the play they may see later. That is part of the enduring power of this remarkable work, which many critics have called Shakespeare's greatest.

As it was for many others, the initial *Hamlet* experience for British actor and Shakespearean scholar Michael Pennington was Laurence Olivier's 1948 film of the play. This visually brooding, energetically staged and acted work won the Academy Award for best picture of the year (as well as one for Olivier as best actor in the title role). Since then, Pennington has seen innumerable Hamlets and has himself played Hamlet on several occasions. And yet, he says, "When I think of Hamlet, I still think of Olivier, because he was my first." The atmospheric black and white photography remains unforgettable, Pennington recalls. "This was done to save money, but was thought to reflect the bleak northern [European] tones of the play, which in fact it did." Most of all, Pennington remembers being mesmerized by the ghost of Hamlet's dead father, "a billowing amoebic [irregularly formed] figure, its face . . . obscure, its heart thumping in the battlement mists." [1]

It is not surprising that Olivier's *Hamlet* remains one of Pennington's favorite versions. "Most people's favorite Hamlets are their first experiences of the play," comments renowned British actor Alec Guinness, "which means they are probably young and it is to the young (with questioning

16

minds) that the character [most] appeals."[2] Indeed, Pennington was only thirteen when he saw Olivier's film. At the time, like other impressionable young people, he thought that the great actor's specific line readings, gestures, and general approach to the part constituted *the* way to play Hamlet; and this must be precisely the way Shakespeare had intended it. Later Pennington learned that this was only one of a seemingly endless number of ways to approach this mammoth and often mysterious role. Actors, directors, and scholars continue to argue (and likely always will) about the character's personality and motivations.

Why, for instance, when Hamlet suspects that his uncle has killed his father to marry his mother, does he not act immediately and decisively? Does he truly love his girlfriend, Ophelia, or is he only using her? When reciting the famous "To be or not to be" speech, is he actually contemplating suicide or just venting his frustrations? Does he have repressed sexual feelings for his mother, Queen Gertrude? Does he really go mad, or is he just faking it? Everyone who approaches Hamlet has his or her own answers to these and other such questions. Collectively, these questions make up what scholars frequently refer to as the "Hamlet problem," which hovers perpetually and menacingly over the role and inevitably haunts all those who endeavor to play it. Thus, there are as many different interpretations of Hamlet and his dilemma as there are productions of the play. And there will always be *Hamlet* initiates, newcomers both on stage and in the audience, to ponder and offer fresh solutions for the Hamlet problem.

A FERTILE CREATIVE ATMOSPHERE FOR A YOUNG PLAYWRIGHT

A widespread misconception has arisen over the years that a similar air of elusiveness and obscurity surrounds the man who created Hamlet. In what might be termed the "Shakespeare problem," the great playwright's life has been portrayed as largely mysterious and undocumented, suggesting to some that he never really existed and fueling numerous attempts to prove that someone else wrote his plays. However, for a common person of the Elizabethan period (ranging from the late 1500s to the early 1600s), Shakespeare's life is unusually *well* documented. The evidence consists of over one hundred official documents, including entries about him and his relatives in parish registers and town archives, legal records involving property transfers, and business letters to or about him. There are also more than fifty allusions to him and his works in the published writings of his contemporaries. Although these sources do not tell us much about Shakespeare's personality, likes and dislikes, and personal beliefs, they provide enough information to piece together a concise outline of the important events in his life.

Shakespeare was born in Stratford, now called Stratford-upon-Avon, a village in Warwickshire County in central England, in 1564. The exact day is somewhat uncertain but tradition accepts it as April 23. If this date is indeed correct, it is an unusual coincidence, for April 23 is celebrated in England as St. George's Day, in honor of the country's patron saint, and is also the documented month and day of Shakespeare's own death fifty-two years later.

Shakespeare was born in a particularly crucial historical time and place—namely England in the last decades of the sixteenth century. This proved to be one of the richest, most dynamic, and most opportune cultural and professional settings for aspiring poets and dramatists in all of Western history. A bevy of great and famous writers, among them Francis Bacon, Christopher Marlowe, Ben Jonson, and John Donne, were all born within a dozen years of Shakespeare's birth and published works during his lifetime. Plays were gaining popularity as legitimate art forms, as evidenced partly by the construction of England's first public theater when Shakespeare was twelve. Not long afterward, Raphael Holinshed's *Chronicles of England, Scotlande, and Irelande,* the source for many of Shakespeare's plots, was published.

What is more, Shakespeare was born at a time when powerful European nations like England were greatly expanding their horizons. It was "an era of change and restlessness," remarks Shakespearean scholar Karl Holzknecht.

> Everywhere—in religion, in philosophy, in politics, in science, in literature—new ideas were springing into life and coming into conflict with the established order of things. . . . A whole series of events and discoveries, coming together at the end of the fifteenth century [just preceding the Elizabethan age], transformed . . . many of the institutions and the habits of mind that we call medieval. The gradual break-up of feudalism . . . the discovery of gunpowder and . . . the mariner's compass and the possibility of safely navigating the limitless ocean, the production of paper and the invention of printing, and . . . the Copernican system of astronomy which formulated a new center of the universe—all of these new conceptions had a profound effect upon human thought and became the foundations for intellectual, moral, social, and economic changes which quickly made themselves felt.[3]

To these forces that shaped Europe in the 1500s can be added many important English historical events that occurred during Shakespeare's own lifetime. In 1587, when Shakespeare was about twenty-three, Queen Elizabeth I beheaded her distant relative and rival for the throne, Mary, Queen of Scots. In the following year an English fleet halted an attempted invasion of England by defeating the mighty Spanish Armada. Sir Francis Drake, Sir John Hawkins, and other adventurous English sea captains helped turn the sea lanes into great highways for England's growing naval power; and, in 1607, English settlers founded the colony of Jamestown in Virginia, giving England a foothold in the New World. England's command of the waves brought it commercial success, and its ports and cities became bustling centers of high finance, social life, and the arts. Amid all of this, the theater, increasingly recognized as an art form, provided a fertile creative atmosphere for the efforts and innovations of young playwrights like Ben Jonson and Will Shakespeare.

SHAKESPEARE'S YOUTH

It was, however, not all that apparent at first that the young Shakespeare would become an important contributor to and shaper of this new and growing theater world. At the time of Shakespeare's birth his father, John Shakespeare, was a glover and perhaps also a wool and leather dealer in Stratford, which was far away from the bustling, cosmopolitan London, where most actors, writers, and other artists congregated and worked. The elder Shakespeare also held various community positions, among them ale taster, town councilman, town treasurer, and eventually bailiff, or mayor. John and his wife, Mary Arden, were married shortly before Queen Elizabeth I's accession to the English throne in 1558; they subsequently produced eight children, of whom William was the third child and eldest son.

Nothing is known about William Shakespeare's childhood, but it is fairly certain that between the ages of seven and sixteen he attended the town grammar school. There, students studied Latin grammar and literature, including the works of the Roman writers Terence, Cicero, Virgil, and Ovid, as well as works by later European authors such as the Dutch moralist Erasmus. In addition to these formal studies, Shakespeare must have done much reading on his own time when in his teens and twenties. We know this because his works reveal a knowledge not only of Latin but also of French and several other languages. Shakespeare was also well versed in both ancient and recent European history, as shown by his intimate familiarity with the *Parallel Lives* of the first-century A.D. Greek writer Plutarch and the works of Holinshed and other English chroniclers.[4] Shakespeare read a great deal of fiction, too, including the classic works of Italy's Giovanni Boccaccio and England's Geoffrey Chaucer.

In addition, and perhaps most importantly, Shakespeare amassed a huge body of practical knowledge about life. He knew the "ins and outs" of the royal court, the trades, the army, the church, and the mannerisms and aspirations of people of all ages and walks of life. The eighteenth-century English novelist Henry Fielding described him as "learned in human nature,"[5] and, indeed, Shakespeare was certainly a supremely educated individual, even if most of what he knew was self-taught.

The first certain fact about Shakespeare after his birth was his wedding, which his marriage license dates November 27, 1582. His bride, who was eight years his senior, was Anne Hathaway, the daughter of a farmer from the nearby village of Shottery. Local documents reveal a daughter, Susanna, christened May 26, 1583, and twins, Hamnet and Judith, christened February 26, 1585; other surviving records show that Hamnet died in 1596 at the age of eleven.

EARLY THEATER EXPERIENCES

Although the exact reason that young Will Shakespeare chose the theater as a profession is unknown, certain facts help form an educated guess. Traveling companies of actors came to Stratford occasionally, erected their makeshift wooden stages, and performed the most popular plays of the day. Stratford records indicate such visits from the theatrical troupes the Queen's Men and the Earl of Worcester's Men in 1568 and 1569, when Shakespeare was about five. Perhaps these and later stage shows intrigued Shakespeare enough to send him to London to try his luck in the theater, an event that likely occurred in 1587, the year Mary, Queen of Scots, lost her head. Various undocumented stories have survived about the young man's first professional job. One maintains that he tended horses outside a theater until offered the position of assistant prompter. "Another theory seems more likely," writes Shakespearean scholar François Laroque, namely that

> Shakespeare attached himself to a theatrical company—perhaps the Queen's Men, which happened to have lost one of its

members in a brawl. The young Shakespeare could easily have stepped into his shoes, as experience was not required. Actors learned on the job.[6]

Apparently Shakespeare learned quicker than most. By 1593 he had written *Richard III, The Comedy of Errors,* and *Henry VI, Parts 1, 2,* and *3,* earning him a solid reputation as a playwright and actor in the London theater scene. At first, he did not attach himself exclusively to any specific theatrical company but worked on and off with several, including that of Richard Burbage, the finest and most acclaimed actor of the time. Burbage, four years younger than Shakespeare, became the playwright's close friend and colleague and eventually played the title roles in the original productions of some of his greatest plays, including *Hamlet, Richard III, King Lear,* and *Othello.* During these early years in London, Shakespeare wrote two long poems, *Venus and Adonis* (1593) and *Lucrece* (1594), the only works he ever published himself. Although his plays, like those of other playwrights of the time, were viewed as popular but lowbrow entertainment, these poems established Shakespeare as an accepted and respectable literary figure.

The founding of Lord Chamberlain's Company in 1594 marked an important turning point in Shakespeare's career. This theatrical company performed at all the major theaters of the day, including the Theatre, the Swan, and the Curtain (the famous Globe had not yet been built). Shakespeare joined the group and stayed with it throughout his career. By 1603, when it became known as the King's Servants, it was performing periodically at the royal court and Shakespeare was a shareholder in all company profits.

As a permanent member of the company, Shakespeare had the opportunity to work on a regular basis with the best English actors of the day. In addition to the great Burbage, these included Henry Condell, John Heminge, William Sly, and Will Kempe. Kempe, one of the great comic players of the Elizabethan stage, specialized in broad, slapstick comedy and physical clowning. Evidence suggests that he played the role of Peter, the bumbling servant to the nurse in *Romeo and Juliet,* and Dogberry, the constable in *Much Ado About Nothing.* Over the years Shakespeare wrote a number of comic roles especially for Kempe, among them Costard in *Love's Labour's Lost,* Launce in *The Two Gentlemen of Verona,* and Bottom in *A Midsummer Night's Dream.*

Indeed, from 1594 on Shakespeare devoted most of his

time to writing plays, although he supposedly occasionally took small roles in productions of his and his colleagues' works. According to tradition, for instance, he played the ghost in *Hamlet.* There may have been nothing at all deep or symbolic about his choosing this role; perhaps the company simply needed him to fill in for another actor who had taken ill. Yet it is certainly possible that more weighty or heartfelt feelings were involved, and later Shakespearean devotees have been unable to resist theorizing about such motivations. That Shakespeare played the ghost "seems as charged with poetic relevance as anything in the text of the play," suggest scholars Phyllis Abrahms and Alan Brody.

> It is yet another image of the elusive relationship between illu-sion and reality which is explored so deeply in *Hamlet.* The idea of the "real" creator of the character of Hamlet playing the "illusory" father of the young prince is one that suggests . . . many levels of meaning . . . particularly if we note, too, that Shakespeare's real son, Hamnet, had died during this period and that the Hamlet of the play can never be sure whether the Ghost is real or a projection of his own imagination.[7]

More certain than his reasons for playing the ghost is the fact that between 1594 and 1601 Shakespeare turned out many plays of astonishing variety and quality. A partial list includes the comedies *The Taming of the Shrew, The Two Gentlemen of Verona, The Merry Wives of Windsor,* and *Twelfth Night;* the histories *Richard II, Henry IV, Parts 1* and *2,* and *Henry V;* and the tragedies *Romeo and Juliet, Julius Caesar,* and *Hamlet.*

THE GLOBE'S OPEN-AIR PIT AND ARENA STAGE

Incredibly, in the midst of this enormous output of master-pieces, the playwright managed to find the time for journeys back and forth to rural Stratford and the family and commu-nity obligations centered there. In 1597 he became a local burgess, or council member, by buying New Place, the largest and finest home in the town (the property included two barns and two gardens). Town records show that he later bought other property in the area, confirming that he had by now acquired more than what was then viewed as a com-fortable living.

A significant portion of this large income must have come from Shakespeare's one-eighth share in the profits of the new and very successful Globe Theatre, which opened in 1598. He and his colleagues in Lord Chamberlain's Company had found it difficult to renew their lease at the Theatre and had decided to build their own playhouse. In the short span of

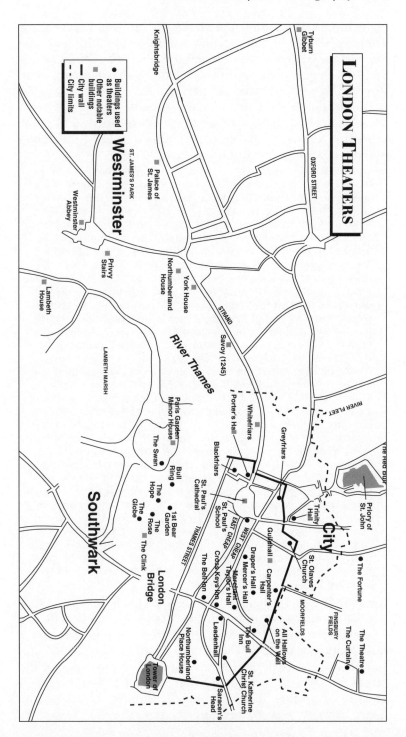

eight months they built the Globe on the south side of the Thames River and entered into a joint ownership deal with Sir Nicholas Brend, who owned the property. This marked the first known instance in theatrical history of actors owning the theater in which they performed.

It was for this theater and the specific properties of its stage that Shakespeare tailored the plays he wrote in the years that followed. That stage, explains Harvard University's noted Shakespearean authority Harry Levin,

> was basically a platform . . . [measuring] 27 1/2 feet deep by 43 feet wide. . . . [It] was encircled on three sides by the standing spectators, or groundlings (who paid a penny for admittance), so that the production—if not quite in the round—employed what today we call arena staging. The surrounding amphitheater . . . consisted of three stories, each with its gallery. . . . Admission to the galleries cost an additional penny and entitled the spectator to a seat. Just beyond [behind] the stage rose the tiring-house, containing—as the name (attiring house) implies—the actors' dressing rooms, and providing a conventionalized background which adapted itself to their histrionic requirements. Most of the acting had to take place downstage [toward the audience]; but upstage there was a curtained area which could be used for discoveries. . . . Behind its curtain . . . which was black for tragedy and parti-colored for comedy . . . would be discovered the body of the slain Polonius [in *Hamlet*] or the sleeping Falstaff [in *The Merry Wives of Windsor*], "snorting like a horse." In the back at a higher level, there was a specialized playing space indicated in the Shakespearean directions as "above" or "aloft.". . . To the left and right of the mainstage were the doors for major exits and entrances. Housed at the highest level were the musicians and the instruments for other sound effects that punctuated the dramatic rhythm. . . . The stage, which stood about five feet from the ground, could be entered from underneath by a trap or traps, whose most famous use was to serve for a grave for Ophelia [in *Hamlet*]. . . . Though the [theater's] large pit was open to the sky, most of the stage was covered by a projecting roof called the "shadow" or "heavens," whose underside was illuminated by signs of the zodiac. . . . Plays had to be performed in broad daylight, of course, between the hours of two and four or five in the afternoon.[8]

It was in the early afternoon, then, that the audience, including the groundlings, entered the theater. The best evidence suggests that the Globe accommodated between two thousand and three thousand spectators in all. Between 1600 and 1607, its open-air pit and arena stage were the scene of the premieres of most of what are now viewed as Shakespeare's greatest tragedies. These included *Hamlet, Othello, King Lear, Macbeth,* and *Antony and Cleopatra.*

LAST WORKS, DEATH, AND POSTHUMOUS HONORS

The eight years that followed these monumental works were the playwright's last. Apparently now secure in his fame and fortune, he seems to have spent much of his time at New Place in Stratford. There, according to various entries in local records and diaries, he became increasingly involved in community and family affairs. He still wrote plays but no longer at the breakneck pace he had maintained in his youth. His last works included *Coriolanus, Pericles, The Winter's Tale, Henry VIII,* and *The Two Noble Kinsmen,* all first performed between 1608 and 1613. *Kinsmen* turned out to be his swan song. He must have become seriously ill in March 1616, for his will was executed on March 25; he died nearly a month later on April 23. The bulk of his estate went to his wife, sister, and daughters Susanna and Judith, although he also left money to some of his theater colleagues, including Richard Burbage.

A few years after Shakespeare's death, a monument to him, designed by Gerard Janssen, was erected in Stratford Church. A greater posthumous honor came in 1623, when two of his former theatrical partners, Henry Condell and John Heminge, published the so-called First Folio, a collection of the playwright's complete plays, under the title *Mr. William Shakespeare's Comedies, Histories, & Tragedies. Published According to the True Original Copies.* The exact nature of these "copies" that served as the Folio's basis remains unclear. Most scholars assume that they were various "quartos," early printed versions of the plays, which the actors often used as performance scripts.

Whatever its sources, the First Folio was extremely important to posterity because it included eighteen plays that had yet to be printed in quarto form and that might otherwise have been lost forever. Among them were some of the playwright's greatest works—*As You Like It, Macbeth, Antony and Cleopatra, The Tempest,* and the great political play, *Julius Caesar.* These works, along with Shakespeare's other plays, Levin writes, have been

> accorded a place in our culture above and beyond their topmost place in our literature. They have been virtually canonized as humanistic scriptures, the tested residue of pragmatic wisdom, a general collection of quotable texts and usable examples. Reprinted, reedited, commented upon, and translated into most languages, they have preempted more space on the library shelves than the books of—or about—any other author. Meanwhile, they have become a staple of the school and

college curricula, as well as the happiest of hunting grounds for scholars and critics.[9]

THE SOURCES FOR *HAMLET*

The "happiest hunting ground" of all, for students, scholars, and critics alike, is undoubtedly *Hamlet.* Shakespeare wrote it in about the year 1600, intending it for a theatrical genre that had recently become very popular in London and other English cities—the "revenge play." A typical revenge play portrayed a hero seeking bloody justice for the wrongful acts of one or more villains and followed a specific formula, as described by noted Shakespearean scholar Norrie Epstein:

> Most of the play consists of the hero's plot to avenge an injustice or a crime committed against a family member. In their obsession with family honor and the violent means they'll take to preserve it, the characters of a revenge play resemble the tightly knit Corleone family in *The Godfather.* A rape, a dismemberment, or an act of incest might add sensationalism, and often a ghost incites the avenger to do his bloody business. By the last act, the stage is usually littered with carnage—much to everyone's delight.[10]

Popular revenge plays that preceded *Hamlet* included *The Spanish Tragedie* (ca. 1586) by English playwright Thomas Kyd and Shakespeare's own *Titus Andronicus* (1593).

The main characters and basic plot of Shakespeare's new revenge play, *Hamlet,* were not his own invention. As a rule, Shakespeare borrowed many of his characters and plots from existing sources, including ancient myths, historical accounts, popular stories, poems, novels, and so on; *Hamlet* was no exception. One of his sources may have been the *Historia Danica* (*Chronicles of the Danish Realm*), a Latin work by the twelfth-century Danish historian Saxo Grammaticus, which tells about a medieval Danish prince named Amlethus.[11] While the prince is still a child, his uncle, Fengon, murders the king, Amlethus's father, and marries the queen, Gerutha. The boy becomes obsessed with getting revenge; because he is still young and relatively powerless, he bides his time, all the while pretending to be mad in order to keep his uncle from discovering his plans for retribution. Nevertheless, Fengon suspects Amlethus is only feigning madness and tries, unsuccessfully, to trick him into lowering his guard. Eventually, the young man sets fire to the castle's great hall and kills the usurper with Fengon's own sword.

Shakespeare may also have been familiar with a 1576 French story based on the earlier Danish work. This French version, which retained many of the characters and events of the original, appeared as one of several tales in the *Histories Tragiques*, by François de Belleforest.[12] Many scholars believe, however, that Shakespeare was most influenced by another work based on the Danish tale, a play performed often in the 1580s and 1590s but subsequently lost. This play, which may have been written by Thomas Kyd, author of *The Spanish Tragedie*, has come to be called the *Ur-Hamlet*.[13] Because the play no longer exists, scholars are unsure of exactly what and how much Shakespeare borrowed from it. The main character in Shakespeare's version is much more introspective and thoughtful and puts off enacting his revenge much longer than the Hamlets in the Danish and French versions. Were these enhancements, which gave the character so much added dimension, the innovations of Shakespeare or of the author of the *Ur-Hamlet*? No one can say for sure.

THE QUARTOS AND FIRST PERFORMANCE

Scholars know quite a bit more about the various early quartos of the play. The First Quarto appeared in 1603 with the title *The Tragical History of Hamlet, Prince of Denmark, by William Shakespeare* and the added subtitle of "As it hath been divers times acted by His Highness' servants in the city of London, as also in the two universities of Cambridge and Oxford and elsewhere." Only about half as long as the later versions, the First Quarto is full of errors and most scholars have come to view it as unreliable; therefore they often refer to it as the "bad quarto." The consensus of opinion is that this corrupted version was reconstructed from memory by one or more actors who had been in a previous production of the play. The Second Quarto, printed in 1604, bore a new subtitle— "Newly imprinted and enlarged to almost as much again as it was, according to the true and perfect copy." Because a majority of scholars suspect that the "perfect copy" was Shakespeare's own original manuscript, they usually refer to the Second Quarto as the "good quarto." The third important early version of *Hamlet* appeared in the 1623 First Folio of the author's works. This one has some eighty-five lines not found in the Second Quarto; but the third version also lacks about two-hundred of the good quarto's lines. Most modern editions of the play use various combinations of the Second Quarto and First Folio versions.

As was the usual procedure at the time, a play's quartos

were published well after the play had already been performed in public. The date of *Hamlet*'s first production is uncertain and might have been as early as 1598 or as late as 1602. The most likely period is 1600–1601, based partly on clues within the text itself. In act 2, scene 2, for example, Hamlet asks the courtier Rosencrantz why the actors visiting the castle are traveling around rather than appearing in their own theater. Rosencrantz asserts that professional actors are out of favor because of "an eyrie [nest] of children" who "berattle [berate] the common [public] stages." This is a direct reference to the so-called "War of the Theaters," which took place between 1599 and 1601. During these years, private theaters using inexperienced child actors competed with and threatened the livelihoods of the more professional public playhouses like those in which Shakespeare worked.

Whenever the first performance of *Hamlet* took place, there is no doubt whatsoever about who played the title role. It was Shakespeare's friend and colleague, Richard Burbage, who, by all accounts, was one of the greatest actors of the Elizabethan age. It is interesting to note that Burbage is said to have weighed some 235 pounds. This seems to corroborate the queen's line in act 5, scene 2, in which, seeing her son dueling, she remarks, "He's fat and scant of breath." Over the centuries, however, most, if not all, Hamlets have been slim; so both actors and scholars have tended to interpret the line to mean "out of shape" or "out of practice," rather than physically plump.

SOME FAMOUS HAMLETS

The list of actors who have succeeded Burbage in the much-coveted role of Hamlet is a distinguished one. Another great Elizabethan player, Joseph Taylor, became the role's chief interpreter when Burbage died in 1619. In 1663, Thomas Betterton began playing Hamlet and continued to do so until 1709, when he was in his seventies. An August 1668 entry in the journal of the noted English diarist Samuel Pepys tells how he went "to the Duke of York's playhouse, and saw 'Hamlet,' which we have not seen this year before, or more; and [we were] mightily pleased with it, but above all with Betterton, the best part, I believe, that ever man acted."[14] A portrait of Betterton in the part, which still hangs in a London theatrical club, shows him in the dark and somber attire that thereafter became associated with the character.

The eighteenth century also had its share of notable Ham-

lets. One of the greatest was David Garrick, who began playing the part in 1742 and whose atmospheric performance is
described in Henry Fielding's 1749 novel *Tom Jones*. In 1783,
John Philip Kemble began playing Hamlet. His contribution
to the role's interpretive evolution was a heavy emphasis on
the character's gloominess and madness. The same century
also witnessed the first important Hamlet in America, Lewis
Hallam, who presented the play in Philadelphia in 1759.

Following in this tradition, some powerful nineteenth-
century American actors tackled the role of Hamlet. Among
the greatest of the century was Edwin Booth (whose brother,
John Wilkes Booth, also an actor, assassinated Abraham Lin-
coln). About Booth's stately performance, a reviewer for the
Atlantic Monthly wrote in 1866:

> Where a burlier tragedian must elaborately pose himself for
> the youth he would assume, this actor so easily and constantly
> falls into beautiful attitudes and movements, that he seems to
> go about, as we heard a humorist say, "making statues all over
> the stage." No picture can equal the scene where Horatio and
> Marcellus swear by his sword, he holding the crossed hilt up-
> right between the two, his head thrown back and lit with high
> resolve [emphasized to great effect].[15]

Other great nineteenth-century Hamlets included the renowned
British actors Sir Henry Irving and Sir Johnston Forbes-
Robertson. A notable addition, in one of the most controversial
portrayals of the role in the period, was the famous actress Sarah
Bernhardt, who appeared in an 1899 Paris production of *Hamlet*.

Many well-known actors carried on the Hamlet performance tradition in the twentieth century, both on stage and
in the new and powerful visual art form of film. One of the
most acclaimed and probably the most influential Hamlet interpretation of the century was that of British actor John
Gielgud, who first played the role at London's Old Vic Theatre
in 1929. Gielgud emphasized the Danish prince's nobility
and restraint. His Hamlet was a sensitive, intellectual, introspective man who preferred to refrain from shouting and violent gestures. "Gielgud's view of the chief character," writes
University of Arizona scholar Mary Z. Maher,

> his mode of playing, and much of his stage business set the fash-
> ion for Hamlets in the decades to come. As a model for others,
> Gielgud cannot be overestimated. Here, indeed, was a definitive
> Hamlet. . . . It was a performance which combined highlighted
> theatrical moments with the psychological realism of an inter-
> nally tormented man trapped in a web of circumstantial events.
> His tears . . . elicited pity and secured the compassion of his audi-
> ence. . . . Gielgud truly was "the glass of fashion and the mold of

form" through which modern Hamlets mirrored themselves.[16]

In 1964, Gielgud approached the play from another angle when he directed Richard Burton, another memorable Hamlet, in a long-running and well-received New York production. Other notable twentieth-century Hamlets included Maurice Evans, John Barrymore, Alec Guinness, Laurence Olivier (in London in 1937 and in the 1948 film), David Warner, Christopher Plummer (in the 1964 TV production shot on location at Elsinore Castle in Denmark), Nicol Williamson (in the 1969 film), Mel Gibson (in the 1990 film), and Kenneth Branagh (in the 1997 film).

SEARCHING FOR THE CHARACTER'S "CENTER"

All of these actors, however different their appearance, mannerisms, vocal and physical interpretations, and so forth, had one important thing in common. Each tried to find the "core" or "center" of the character, to tackle and perhaps solve one or more of the various aspects of the "Hamlet problem" that have captivated and bewildered both players and spectators since Burbage's day. In so doing, each had to confront the reality that both the character and the play revolve around a relentless preoccupation with getting violent revenge.

Gielgud suggested that such violence was not in Hamlet's nature. He saw the character as a gentle man trapped in circumstances beyond his control and therefore forced, against his will and better judgment, to enact revenge. In this and other similar interpretations, the character has no close friends, no one to confide in or to guide him. Thus, he makes up his mind about what to do by talking to himself in soliloquies (speeches recited when alone). As it happens, the decisions he makes unfortunately lead to many deaths, including his own.

While Gielgud's Hamlet is harried and coerced by external forces, Olivier's controversial prince, by contrast, is driven by internal forces, specifically dark and bizarre ones. In approaching the role, Olivier was influenced by the ideas of two famous early-twentieth-century psychoanalysts, Sigmund Freud and Ernest Jones. They concluded that Hamlet suffers from an Oedipus complex, a repressed hatred for his dead father and sexual desire for his mother, Queen Gertrude. In this view, Hamlet delays killing his uncle, Claudius, and thereby getting his revenge, because subconsciously he wants the same thing Claudius does, namely Gertrude. On some level the young man realizes that he is no better than his uncle; if he kills Claudius, he must also rid the world of himself. In his film of the play, Olivier emphasized Hamlet's repressed feelings for the queen by increasing the duration of the kisses between mother and son and having the camera linger suggestively on Gertrude's bed.[17]

Another controversial Hamlet, played by David Warner in Britain's 1966 Royal Shakespeare Company production, took a completely different approach. Following director Peter Hall's concept, Warner played the prince as a young, idealistic nonconformist, a rebel very much like the "new left," antiestablishment youth that came to be identified with the 1960s. The hippies and other new left radicals were impatient with their elders and disillusioned by rampant political and social corruption. Warner's Hamlet is similarly disillusioned by the corrupt establishment at Elsinore, which can be "cleansed" only by the prince's honesty and righteous sense of outrage; but alas, he finds himself unable to act. As Hall puts it, Hamlet's disillusionment

> produces an apathy of the will so deep that commitment to politics, to religion or to life is impossible. For a man said to do nothing, Hamlet does a great deal. . . . He is always on the brink of action, but something inside him, this disease of disillusionment, stops the final, committed action.[18]

A UNIVERSAL APPEAL AND FASCINATION

That these and many other diverse interpretations are not only possible but also theoretically valid is what makes Shakespeare's achievement in writing *Hamlet* so great. How did he create a play and a character so relevant and appealing to all ages and cultures? Essentially, he took a popular but tired formula of his own age, the revenge play, and superimposed on it a gripping psychological drama about a man tortured by indecision. Should Hamlet take the "natural" but "uncivilized" action of enacting his revenge? Or, should he find some other, less violent, and therefore more civilized way of dealing with his grief and anger? His indecision about which avenue to take is what causes his celebrated delay in completing his revenge.

People everywhere can relate to such a dilemma. At some point, almost everyone has faced making a choice, knowing that whichever option is selected will forever alter his or her life. And those at such critical junctures have often found themselves, at least momentarily, paralyzed by indecision. Perhaps this is a factor that makes the character and the play so universally appealing and fascinating. As Michael Pennington astutely observes:

> One of the reasons audiences admire the play so much is that everybody in their own lives . . . faces the kind of crisis that Hamlet faces, that is, do you behave like a reactive [emotion-driven] savage or like a rational and sensitive human being?[19]

People everywhere also readily understand Hamlet's disillusionment with and bitterness about the unhappy turns his life has taken; for momentary feelings of despair and hopelessness are ever-present facets of the human condition. "I have of late—but wherefore [why] I know not—lost all my mirth," Hamlet says in act 2, scene 2. "It goes so heavily with my disposition [feelings, nature]," he continues, "that this goodly frame, the earth, seems to me a sterile promontory [bleak landscape]." The air and the sky, which he calls "a majestical roof fretted with golden fire [i.e., the sun]," should fill him with wonder and joy. But instead, it appears to him "a foul and pestilent congregation of vapors." He follows these remarks with a brief, magnificently worded query about human nature and worth that, in varying forms, has been asked throughout the ages. We are told that a human being is a wonderful and special creation, Hamlet says in essence; but in reality, might we be nothing but spiritless matter and our lives ultimately meaningless?

> What a piece of work is a man! how noble in reason! how infinite in faculties! in form and moving how express and admirable! in action how like an angel! in apprehension how like a god! the beauty of the world, the paragon [most perfect example] of animals! And yet to me what is this quintessence [basic underlying nature] of dust?

Perhaps part of what makes Shakespeare's melancholy Dane a character for all times is that he asks some of the more profound and soul-searching questions that have always intrigued and will no doubt always continue to haunt the human race.

NOTES

1. Michael Pennington, Hamlet: *A User's Guide.* New York: Proscenium, 1996, pp. 4–5.
2. Quoted in Mary Z. Maher, *Modern Hamlets and Their Soliloquies.* Iowa City: University of Iowa Press, 1992, p. 22.
3. Karl J. Holzknecht, *The Backgrounds of Shakespeare's Plays.* New York: American, 1950, pp. 33–34.
4. The characters and events Shakespeare depicted in his political play *Julius Caesar,* for example, were drawn directly

from Plutarch's biographies of Caesar, Brutus, and Antony; and Holinshed's *Chronicles* was an important source for the plots of his English history plays.

5. Quoted in Harry Levin, introduction to *The Riverside Shakespeare*. Boston: Houghton and Mifflin, 1974, p. 4.
6. François Laroque, *The Age of Shakespeare.* New York: Harry N. Abrams, 1993, p. 39.
7. Phyllis Abrahms and Alan Brody, introduction to *Hamlet,* ed. Michael Martin. New York: Prestige Books, 1968, p. xxx.
8. Levin, *The Riverside Shakespeare*, pp. 15–16.
9. Levin, *The Riverside Shakespeare*, p. 1.
10. Norrie Epstein, *The Friendly Shakespeare: A Thoroughly Painless Guide to the Best of the Bard.* New York: Viking Penguin, 1993, p. 308.
11. The name Hamlet is a form of Amleth, the non-Latinized version of Amlethus.
12. Belleforest's work was translated into English by Thomas Pavier as *The Hystorie of Hamblet* in 1608, about seven or eight years after Shakespeare wrote his own version; but Shakespeare may have read the story in the original French sometime in the 1580s or 1590s.
13. The prefix "Ur" is a reference to the ancient Mesopotamian city of Ur, one of the first known human cities; its use in this manner usually denotes an "earlier" or "ancestral" version of something. The classic modern study of this vanished play and the possible identity of its author appears in Fredson T. Bowers, *Elizabethan Revenge Tragedy, 1587–1642.* Princeton, NJ: Princeton University Press, 1940.
14. Quoted in Samuel Thurber and A.B. de Mille, eds., *Hamlet.* Boston: Allyn and Bacon, 1922, p. 169.
15. Quoted in Martin, *Hamlet,* p. xxxii.
16. Maher, *Modern Hamlets,* pp. 2, 18.
17. Freud first proposed this theory in 1897. Later, Jones, a Freudian disciple, published articles elaborating on it. The most complete and detailed treatment is Jones's 1949 book *Hamlet and Oedipus* (New York: W.W. Norton). Also see M.D. Faber, *The Design Within: Psychoanalytic Approaches to Shakespeare* (New York: Science House, 1970), for extracts from and discussions of the Shakespearean ideas of Freud and Jones.
18. Quoted in Maher, *Modern Hamlets,* p. 43.
19. Quoted in Epstein, *The Friendly Shakespeare,* p. 343.

CHAPTER 1

The Plot, Structure, Setting, and Wordplay of *Hamlet*

The Story Told in *Hamlet*

Marchette Chute

The story told in Shakespeare's *Hamlet*, which contains many of the important elements of the original Danish chronicle on which it was based, is one of the most famous in world literature. This summary of the plot is by Marchette Chute, one of the twentieth century's leading American authorities on English literary history.

The story opens in the cold and dark of a winter night in Denmark, while the guard is being changed on the battlements of the royal castle of Elsinore. For two nights in succession, just as the bell strikes the hour of one, a ghost has appeared on the battlements, a figure dressed in complete armor and with a face like that of the dead king of Denmark, Hamlet's father. A young man named Horatio, who is a school friend of Hamlet, has been told of the apparition and cannot believe it, and one of the officers has brought him there in the night so that he can see it for himself.

The hour comes, and the ghost walks. The awed Horatio tries to speak to it but it stalks away, leaving the three men to wonder why the buried king has come back to haunt the land. It may be because his country is in danger, for there is a threat of war in Denmark; the nephew of the king of Norway is talking of invading it. Whatever the message is that has wakened the ghost, it refuses to share it with them. But perhaps it will speak to Hamlet, and they decide to go and tell the dead king's son what they have seen that night.

HAMLET'S SENSE OF ANGUISH AND OUTRAGE

Hamlet is in one of the great ceremonial rooms of the castle, somberly watching the behavior of his uncle. His uncle is now king of Denmark, for he has married Hamlet's mother and as-

From *Stories from Shakespeare*, by Marchette Chute. Copyright 1956 by E.P. Dutton. Copyright renewed 1984 by Marchette Chute. Reprinted by permission of Elizabeth Hauser.

cended the throne of Hamlet's father. . . . Hamlet is still wearing black in mourning for his father's death, and his uncle chides him gently for what he feels is an undue show of grief. But the king can get no answer from Hamlet, who throws him one brief sentence and then addresses all his remarks to his mother; and it is his mother, the queen, who persuades him not to go back to the university again but to stay at Elsinore.

The royal pair and their courtiers leave the room, and Hamlet is left alone, to face the sick disgust that he has felt all through the conversation. . . .

It is not only his father's sudden death that has plunged Hamlet so deep in melancholy. It is the even greater shock of his mother's marriage, less than two months later, to a man for whom Hamlet has the most savage personal contempt. He cannot keep his sick imagination from playing about the details of their life together, and his sense of anguish and outrage deepens the more his mind dwells on it.

Horatio enters, together with the two officers of the watch, and Hamlet welcomes him delightedly. . . . Horatio tells him that the ghost of his dead father has returned to haunt the battlements, and Hamlet is profoundly stirred. "Indeed, indeed, sirs, but this troubles me." He arranges to meet the three of them that night, to watch for the ghost's return, and then waits longingly for the darkness.

A WORLD OF GHOSTS AND GOBLINS

The son of the lord chamberlain, a young man named Laertes, makes his final preparations to leave for France and gives his sister a few last-minute instructions before he goes. Her name is Ophelia, and Hamlet has been paying court to her. In Laertes' opinion, she should not pay too much attention to the prince's talk of love for he is heir to the throne of Denmark and not free to marry where he pleases. Ophelia is a gentle girl, very strictly brought up, and she promises to conduct herself carefully at home if he will do the same in Paris.

Their father the chamberlain enters, a pompous, talkative old man whose name is Polonius. He has gathered together a long string of moral maxims to guide his son on his travels, and after Laertes leaves he turns to Ophelia. In the opinion of Polonius also she has been seeing too much of the prince, and although Ophelia maintains that Hamlet . . . intends marriage, her father gives her an outright order that she is to see no more of him.

Horatio and Hamlet meet on the battlements near midnight. They wait in the cold and darkness, and . . . the ghost suddenly enters. Hamlet is jerked into a world that has nothing to do with calm intelligence and careful reasoning, a world of ghosts and goblins and of a forced return from the gates of hell. His father has come out of his grave, and Hamlet searches wildly for words with which to speak to him. . . .

The ghost turns and speaks, and it is then that Hamlet receives the full weight of a hideous discovery. For the king his father did not die a natural death. He was poisoned by his brother, who stole his life, his crown and his queen; and a murderer now reigns in Denmark. The dead king has returned from his own torment in purgatory to ask his son to avenge the murder, and to ask him also not to hurt his mother, the woman all three men love. "Leave her to heaven."

The ghost vanishes, leaving Hamlet shaken almost to hysteria by his hatred of his uncle. "O villain, villain, smiling, damnèd villain!" He has not been told what form his revenge ought to take. He only knows that from this time forward it must be the center of his life. He sees himself—that subtle, intelligent, civilized man—as a single rigid instrument dedicated only to vengeance. . . . Hamlet . . . tries to make the three men swear that they will not reveal what they have seen and heard that night. . . .

The three men swear on the hilt of Hamlet's sword that they will reveal nothing; and, if he behaves strangely about the court, they will not suggest they know why. . . .

Hamlet Insane?

Polonius, the lord chamberlain, has been puttering about in his secretive way, making sure that his children obey all his precepts that have been given them. He sets a servant to spy on his son's behavior in Paris, in the calm conviction he is doing it only for his son's good, and it is for his daughter's good that he has ordered her to see no more of Hamlet. The frightened Ophelia comes in to tell her father that Hamlet broke in upon her while she sat sewing. With his face as white as his shirt and the look of a man who had seen hell, he gripped her wrist, stared at her face as intently as though he were memorizing it, and then backed out of the room with his eyes never leaving hers. Polonius, much shocked by this unforeseen development, decides that Hamlet has been driven insane by unrequited love. He deeply regrets he ever told his daughter to spurn the prince and trots off to tell the news to the king.

The king is already very much aware of the change in Hamlet's behavior, and extremely worried by it. He has asked two friends of Hamlet's youth to come to the court—Rosencrantz and Guildenstern—in the hope that they can find out what is troubling the prince. The king has at least the consolation of good news from Norway, for the prince of that country has given up all thought of invading Denmark and merely wants safe passage for a military expedition farther south. Polonius enters with a long-winded explanation of his private theories about Hamlet, and the queen is inclined to believe them. The king is not so sure, but he agrees to set a watch on Hamlet's behavior when he is with Ophelia. . . .

"THE PLAY'S THE THING"!

[Later] Rosencrantz and Guildenstern come in, and Hamlet does not have the contempt for them he does for the lord chamberlain. He lets them see a little of the heaviness of his heart and calls Denmark a prison. The two men protest that it is not, but Hamlet has learned a deeper truth. . . .

Hamlet makes the two men admit that the king has sent them, and then gives them an answer to take back: his trouble is only melancholy. He makes a most eloquent speech on the beauty and wonder of the world and why it seems only a heap of grayness to him. Even man, that incredible and intricate piece of creation, is to him only a "quintessence of dust. Man delights not me; no, nor woman either, though by your smiling you seem to say so."

The two men hurriedly explain that they smiled only to think what a poor welcome Hamlet would give to the troupe of traveling actors who have come to Elsinore, and Hamlet is instantly delighted to know that the players have arrived. His quick mind, which leaps at everything, wants to know how they have prospered since he saw them last, and when the players themselves appear Hamlet greets them as old friends. . . . Hamlet detains one of the actors for a moment and asks him to present a play called "The Murder of Gonzago" before the king with a few extra lines to be written into the text by Hamlet himself.

Then Hamlet is left alone, and the courteous, witty, intelligent young prince dissolves into a tormented human being. . . .

He cannot be sure what he ought to do. It may very well be that the ghost was an evil spirit, tempting him to his own destruction by telling lies, and Hamlet must have proof of his uncle's guilt before he has a right to take revenge. Tomorrow night, at the play, a scene of murder by poison will be presented by the actors whom Hamlet has trained; and if his uncle turns pale, the dead man's son will know what to do.

> The play's the thing
> Wherein I'll catch the conscience of the king.

To Die or Not to Die?

Rosencrantz and Guildenstern report to the king that they have not been able to find the real reason for Hamlet's behavior, and the king turns to his second source of information, Ophelia. Her father sets her out, with a book in her hand, in a place where Hamlet is sure to come, and then he and the king hide themselves to watch what will happen.

Hamlet enters, desperate enough by this time to be thinking of suicide. It seems to him that it would be such a sure way of escape from torment, just to cease existing, and he gives the famous speech on suicide that has never been worn thin by repetition. "To be, or not to be . . ." It would be easy to stop living.

> To die, to sleep;
> No more. And by a sleep to say we end
> The heartache and the thousand natural shocks
> That flesh is heir to . . .

But Hamlet has never succeeded in deceiving himself, and he cannot do so now. . . .

[He] will not . . . be able to kill himself. He has thought too much about it to be able to take any action.

He sees Ophelia, who has been holding some little gifts he gave her in the days when he also gave her his love. She wants to give them back to him, and Hamlet, in his turn, wants nothing to do with any woman. His mother has given herself to a murderer, and everything about the idea of marriage sickens him. . . . He lashes out at Ophelia as wildly as though she has invented the propagation of the human race, so full of pain himself that he cannot stop to be aware of the pain he is causing, and she can only conclude that Hamlet is hopelessly insane.

The listening king is not so easily deceived. He knows that Hamlet has something definite on his mind and is afraid it may threaten his own safety. Hamlet must be sent out of the country, and the king is easily able to think of a political excuse to send him to England. . . .

THE DEATH OF POLONIUS

Hamlet is very much occupied with his production of the play and is full of advice to the players on the art of acting. It is only to Horatio that he tells his basic purpose, and he asks his friend to watch the king's face during the poisoning scene. The king and queen and all the courtiers enter to see the show, and Hamlet, as restless as a cat, lies down at Ophelia's feet and talks more than he should.

"The Murder of Gonzago" begins, and the king grows increasingly disturbed. Hamlet assures him that the whole thing is mere make-believe. . . . The actual scene of the poisoning comes, and the king sees a re-enactment of his own crime. He can endure it no longer. He rises and calls for lights, and the performance ends in confusion. Hamlet is wild with excitement at the success of his plan, and when he receives word that his mother wants to speak to him, he goes with the conviction that now he can be firm in the "bitter business" he has vowed to perform. . . .

Polonius has gone to the queen's room, since he intends to report back to the king everything that Hamlet says, and he is giving her some final instructions when they hear Hamlet coming. Polonius hides behind the wall hanging, and Hamlet enters the room so tense with fury that the queen thinks for a moment her son intends to murder her. She calls out for help and Polonius echoes her; and Hamlet, thinking it is the king, drives his sword through the tapestry. Then he discovers that he has killed the silly old man instead. . . .

Hamlet has no interest in Polonius at the moment. His whole soul is focused on his mother, intent on making her acknowledge her sin. The bewildered woman can understand nothing in his words except the violence in them, and when he suddenly begins to talk to the empty air she is more convinced than ever that he must be mad. . . .

The queen tells her husband that Hamlet has killed Polonius in a fit of insanity, and the king sends Rosencrantz and Guildenstern to find where Hamlet has hidden the body. Hamlet will not tell anyone where he has been able to "lug the guts," as he calls it, and his behavior is so wild that the king has no difficulty in justifying his own plan. For Rosencrantz and Guildenstern bear letters to England demanding the death of Hamlet as soon as he arrives there.

OPHELIA'S DEMISE AND FUNERAL

On his way to England, Hamlet encounters the army of the prince of Norway, who is passing through Denmark on his way to Poland. . . .

[Meanwhile] her father's death has been too much for the gentle, sheltered spirit of Ophelia, and she wanders through the court singing songs she should never have heard or known. She is insane, and the king and queen can only watch her in helpless pity.

Her brother Laertes, when he hears the news, takes a different course. He is sure that it was the king who murdered his father, and he promptly raises the standard of revolt. The king knows exactly how to handle a hasty young man and has no difficulty in persuading Laertes that Hamlet should be the object of his rage. It takes the king a little longer to persuade Laertes to murder Hamlet, but he finally agrees to challenge him to a duel and kill him with a poisoned rapier.

The king is obliged to hurry, for Hamlet has slipped out of the trap that was laid for him in England. He sends word to the king that he is coming home, but he knows nothing of what has been happening in his absence. Above all, he does not know that Ophelia is no longer living. She tried to hang a wreath on a willow tree near a brook, and when the branch broke with her weight she made no effort to save herself. Instead she lay in the water, singing her little songs, until she drowned.

Ophelia is to be buried in the churchyard, and two very chatty gravediggers prepare her grave. . . . One of them remains behind to finish the grave, and Hamlet arrives to find him singing to himself, as cheerfully insensitive to death as the clods of earth he is flinging about.

Hamlet is in no special hurry to return to the court, and the gravedigger and the loose bones fascinate him. He finds the skull of a jester he loved when he was a small boy, a man named Yorick, and his quick imagination begins to range over the whole subject of the dissolution of the human body . . . when a funeral procession approaches and he lingers to see whose it is.

It is the funeral of Ophelia, attended by all the court, and her brother Laertes is half-crazed with grief. . . . His ranting suddenly puts Hamlet into "a towering passion" and he leaps into the grave to shout even louder than Laertes. . . .

HAMLET'S END

Back in the castle, Hamlet can feel only the most profound regret for his behavior in the graveyard. "I forgot myself." He resolves to make a special effort to be a friend to Laertes, and when a mincing courtier brings a challenge from him, Hamlet teases the courtier a little but accepts the challenge. He believes it is only a friendly bout, and yet he admits to Horatio that he feels a foreboding. . . .

The court gathers to watch the fencing match between the two young men, and only the king and Laertes know that both the rapier and the wine are poisoned. Hamlet begins by offering Laertes his full apologies, with the courtesy that is always his when his shaken soul can give it time to show itself, and the last scene of his life begins.

The end comes quickly. Hamlet scores the first and second hits, and the king tries to persuade him to stop and drink a little wine. Hamlet, intent on the match, puts the cup aside, and the queen picks it up and drinks it. The king, knowing it is poisoned, tries too late to stop her, and she falls dying just as her son and his opponent are both hurt by the poisoned sword. It has changed hands in a close scuffle, and Laertes knows that he deserves his coming death. "I am justly killed with mine own treachery." He manages to gasp out the whole of the plot to Hamlet, ending with the final cry, "The king, the king's to blame."

The dying Hamlet seizes the poisoned sword with his own blood still upon it, stabs the king and then forces the poisoned wine down his throat. The courtiers stand aghast and he tries to tell them what has happened, for even with death closing in upon him he can still remember that he is prince of Denmark and responsible for the welfare of his country. But he no longer has the strength and he leaves the task to Horatio, with the final wish that the prince of Norway is to rule Denmark. He has no more to say. "The rest is silence."

Horatio gives a last heartbroken farewell to the lonely, tormented, incomparable human being he loved so much.

> Good-night, sweet prince,
> And flights of angels sing thee to thy rest.

Four captains carry Hamlet's body away to give it a soldier's burial, and there is a military salute to the dead prince of Denmark as the play ends.

Hamlet and the Elizabethan Revenge Tragedy Formula

Phyllis Abrahms and Alan Brody

From both thematic and structural standpoints, *Hamlet* is part of the revenge play tradition that was popular in the English theater in the late 1500s and early 1600s. Thus, it contains most, if not all, of the standard elements of the formula such plays routinely followed. Among these are ghosts calling out for retribution, disguises and feigned madness as tools by the main character, one or more scheming kings (or queens), politicians, or military leaders who cause murder and mayhem, and a long string of deaths, both of the villains and the tormented hero. Yet, as University of Hartford scholars Phyllis Abrahms and Alan Brody here point out, Shakespeare used these elements merely as a starting point in creating a drama that brilliantly explores a wide range of human feelings and emotions.

No play demonstrates the power and the glory of Shakespeare's tragic vision more than *Hamlet*, which for over three hundred and fifty years has excited us with its action, its insight, its brilliant language. *Hamlet* is an unparalleled adventure story, complete with suspense, intrigue, murder—even a battle at sea with pirates. It is a play of intense emotional and physical violence. Yet underlying all of this are some of the most profound explorations of the mysteries of human existence. Through his characters and their actions Shakespeare probes the nature of death, of fate, of madness. He reveals the eternal conflicts between reality and illusion, faith and despair, the mind and the body. . . .

There are ten deaths in *Hamlet*, if we include the death of Hamlet's father and the "make-believe" death of the Player-

Reprinted by permission of the authors from Phyllis Abrahms and Alan Brody's Introduction to *Hamlet*, by William Shakespeare, edited by Michael Martin (New York: Prestige Books, 1968).

King. The cause of each can be attributed directly to another character's action—or lack of it. But if a play is to be a coherent work of art there must be some *central* action around which all the other parts revolve. What is the central, unifying action of *Hamlet*?

Revenge.

THE REVENGE TRAGEDY FORMULA

Hamlet is a play in the great tradition of Elizabethan revenge tragedy. This is a form which can be traced back to the Roman dramatist Seneca, whose *Thyestes* allowed its audience to witness the slow, inexorable movement of a plot wholly motivated by that one bloodthirsty passion. Seneca was one of the classical authors most respected in the sixteenth century. His strongly delineated line of action and his ability to drench the stage in gore appealed to the robust Elizabethan temperament.

Seneca, His Tenne Tragedies, was translated into English in 1581 by Thomas Newton, and soon after a spate [large number] of revenge tragedies was written and performed in England. They included *The Spanish Tragedy* by Thomas Kyd, *Antonio's Revenge* by John Marston, *The Revenger's Tragedy* by Cyril Tourneur, and *The Revenge of Bussy D'Ambois* by John Chapman. Chapman contributed his play in 1610. *The Spanish Tragedy* was written about 1586. Between these, somewhere around 1602, came *Hamlet*.

Revenge tragedy follows a rather strict formula; a number of elements are common to all plays of the type. All contain the appearance of a ghost who cries for revenge. In all, the hero must disguise himself in order to obtain the information he needs to justify his acts of revenge. Sometimes he employs physical disguise; more often he feigns madness which threatens to become real. In all, a female character goes mad from excessive grief. In all, the villain is a Machiavellian [scheming, cunning] politician who has murdered for both lust and power. In all, the hero is forced by some circumstance to delay the consummation of his plot. In all, the act of revenge finally demands the death of the revenger as well.

"PRIMITIVE" VERSUS "CIVILIZED"

Hamlet falls into this tradition easily. But it is not enough simply to list the "rules" of revenge tragedy and check them off as they appear in Shakespeare's play. *Hamlet* is a masterpiece not because it conforms to a set of conventions but because it takes those conventions and transmutes them into the pure gold of vital, relevant meaning. Hamlet's feigned madness, for instance, becomes the touchstone for an illumination of the mysterious nature of sanity itself. Ophelia's death is infused with a pathos that suggests the helplessness of all innocent victims caught in the crossfire of a power struggle which they cannot comprehend and which ultimately and senselessly destroys them. The Ghost becomes a rich and compressed symbol of a young man's ambiguous but inescapable fate as his father's son. The unifying action of "primitive" revenge assumes cosmic proportions when revenge becomes the responsibility of as "civilized" a human being as young Hamlet.

A REVENGE PLAY VILLAIN BRAGS ABOUT HIS CRIMES

Like Hamlet, Titus Andronicus *(1593), Shakespeare's first revenge tragedy, contains the basic elements of the Elizabethan revenge genre, including dastardly villains whose evil deeds complicate the plot. In this speech from Act 5, Scene 1 of* Titus, *Aaron, a brutal character allied with the evil queen, Tamora, proudly recounts his bloody deeds.*

Even now I curse the day—and yet I think
Few come within the compass of my curse—
Wherein I did not some notorious ill:
As kill a man, or else devise his death,
Ravish a maid, or plot the way to do it,
Accuse some innocent, and forswear myself,
Set deadly enmity between two friends,
Make poor men's cattle break their necks,
Set fire on barns and haystalks in the night,
And bid the owners quench them with their tears.
Oft have I digg'd up dead men from their graves,
And set them upright at their dear friends' door,
Even when their sorrows almost was forgot,
And on their skins, as on the bark of trees,
Have with my knife carved in Roman letters,
"Let not your sorrow die, though I am dead."
But I have done a thousand dreadful things,
As willingly as one would kill a fly,
And nothing grieves me heartily indeed,
But that I cannot do ten thousand more.

The Riverside Shakespeare. Boston: Houghton and Mifflin, 1974, p. 1046.

The tradition of revenge, then, clearly gave Shakespeare the formal framework within which to build his play. . . .

ONE ACTS QUICKLY, THE OTHER DELAYS

It is important to note how Shakespeare pursues the revenge motif relentlessly through the plot line of his work, for it is out of this pursuit that all the great questions of the play emerge.

Hamlet is a son who must avenge his father's murder. He is killed by Laertes, another son who must avenge his own father's murder. There is a difference, however, between the way these two sons go about their business. Laertes in Act IV, Scene V, rushes into his action as soon as he hears of Polonius's death.

> LAERTES
> How came he dead? I'll not be juggled with.
> To hell allegiance, vows to the blackest devil,
> Conscience and grace to the profoundest pit!
> I dare damnation. To this point I stand,
> That both the worlds I give to negligence,
> Let come what comes, only I'll be revenged
> Most thoroughly for my father.
>
> > KING
> >   Who shall stay you?
>
> > LAERTES
> > My will, not all the world's.

Hamlet in Act II, Scene II, delays.

> HAMLET
> Yet I,
> A dull and muddy-mettled rascal, peak
> Like John-a-dreams, unpregnant of my cause,
> And can say nothing. No, not for a King
> Upon whose property and most dear life
> A damned defeat was made. Am I a coward?

He contemplates suicide; he looks for certainty; he plots; he dissembles; he spies; he acts once and kills the wrong man; he acts again, but only at the end of the play when every other course is closed, and one young girl, her father, her brother, two college friends, Hamlet's mother, and even Hamlet himself have already paid for the delay with their lives.

The Play's Courtly Setting

R.A. Foakes

In this perceptive essay, Shakespearean scholar R.A. Foakes discusses the setting in which Hamlet's tragic story unfolds, specifically the royal court at Denmark's Elsinore Castle. The court's extremely dignified and stately atmosphere, Foakes points out, is both defined and carefully maintained by the formality and bland generality of typical court language. Traditional military and religious images also serve to give Elsinore a stately, pompous air, trappings that, Foakes maintains, attempt to hide the fact that the court is, in a very real way, a prison. Hamlet, his mother (Gertrude), his uncle (Claudius), his girl-friend (Ophelia), and the others appear trapped in this confined little world. And the melancholy prince seeks constantly to break down the prison walls, to see and confront the ugly, often brutal realities lying behind the seemingly mild-mannered courtly appearances.

The court of Elsinore which is the focal point of all the action in Hamlet has a dual character, realized largely by means of style and imagery. The good values of the court are presented through its honour and dignity, through qualities associated with the majesty and eloquence of style in the play; the unpleasant side of the court through the imagery that springs from and extends the significance of the action. These aspects are important in setting the tone and establishing the themes, for they are made actual on the stage from the beginning, and the final revelation of evil is brought about through the conflict between them. Writers on the imagery of Hamlet have given a gloomy picture of the play's atmosphere as one in which poison, disease and cor-

Reprinted from R.A. Foakes, "*Hamlet* and the Court of Elsinore," in *Shakespeare Survey: An Annual Survey of Shakespearian Study and Production*, no. 9, edited by Allardyce Nicoll (Cambridge: Cambridge University Press, 1956), by permission of the publisher.

ruption are 'dominant', this is misleading, for though corruption underlies the play's action, it exists chiefly in Hamlet's imagination: as a result, it is latent rather than actual,
like the murder of Hamlet's father, which is not seen, but remains always in the background. The oppositions between
the honour and the prison-like nature of the court are at
least as important in creating the atmosphere of Hamlet, and
a consideration of them suggests a more balanced picture. . . .

THE FORMALITY OF COURTLY SPEECH

One of the most prominent features of *Hamlet* is the ceremonious and stately diction of the court. When the major
characters speak in public they have generally a leisured
way of speaking, using many words to say little, freely am-
plifying and illustrating, as when . . . Hamlet welcomes the
news that the players are coming:

> He that plays the king shall be welcome; his majesty shall
> have tribute of me; the adventurous knight shall use his foil
> and target; the lover shall not sigh gratis.
>
> (II, ii, 332–5)

This rhetorical way of speaking appears in the devices of
Hamlet's excuse to Laertes, "Was't Hamlet wrong'd Laertes?
Never Hamlet", in the marked pompousness of the verse
Rosencrantz and Guildenstern use for intercourse with the
King, and in the formal balance of such lines as:

> *King.*   Thanks, Rosencrantz and gentle Guildenstern.
> *Queen.* Thanks, Guildenstern and gentle Rosencrantz. . . .
>
> (II, ii, 33–4)

It is a 'public' manner of speaking, which tends to sound
similar in the mouths of different characters, and preserves
an outward stateliness and formality in the court.

While it is more or less habitual to the practised courtiers
like Polonius, Laertes or Osric, it may also afford a screen
behind which truth can be concealed, and there is a strong
contrast between the public and private speech of several
characters, notably Claudius and Hamlet. Claudius, for instance, has a more direct and personal manner when praying, trying to obtain information, or plotting with an accom-
plice, but for the most part he is shown speaking in
public. . . . It is the vice of Polonius that he exaggerates the
worst features of the style, and on this occasion the King and
Queen are eager for fact and have no time for rhetoric;

"More matter, with less art", cries Gertrude.

Other elements in the play contribute to this formal, rhetorical tone. There is endless moralizing. . . . Claudius is ready with long-winded and commonplace advice for Hamlet, and so are Polonius for Laertes, Laertes for Ophelia, and Hamlet for the players. Many characters besides Polonius are stored with proverbs or 'sentences'. Set speeches and formal descriptions abound, such as Horatio's account of events in Denmark, the Ghost's tale of the murder, Hamlet's speech on man, Gertrude's description of Ophelia's death, Hamlet's story of the sea-battle. . . .

All these formal elements are present in some of the 'public' speeches, such as the court flattery of Rosencrantz. The pomp and spaciousness of such diction is part of the atmosphere of *Hamlet*. The court of Elsinore is a place of ostensible stateliness and nobility; affairs of state, dealings with ambassadors, preparations for war, enter into the action, and many of the 'pictures' the play presents on the stage, its direct images, are static or nearly so, like the pictorial effect of the dumb-show in the play scene, of Hamlet's contemplation of Claudius praying, of the pictures in the closet-scene, and of the skulls in the graveyard-scene.

MILITARY AND RELIGIOUS IMAGERY

This dignity is enhanced by the frequent imagery of war, not the hurly-burly, clamour, movement and destruction of war—there are no battles in the play—but war with an air of chivalry, reflected in the personal challenges which old Fortinbras had made to Hamlet's father, and Laertes makes later to Hamlet. War is a pursuit of honour, and the exercise of arms is a courtly accomplishment. 'Honour' governs also in Laertes's quarrel with Hamlet; when Hamlet apologizes, Laertes is "satisfied in nature", but

> in my terms of honour
> I stand aloof; and will no reconcilement,
> Till by some elder masters, of known honour,
> I have a voice and precedent of peace.
>
> (V, ii, 257–60)

There is, too, a very real warlikeness about the state of Denmark; this extends from the opening scene, in which the soldiers standing on guard against possible attack from Norway are startled by the "martial stalk" of the armed Ghost, to the return at the end of the play of Fortinbras "with conquest come from Poland". Imagery of war is common in the language of most characters, of Hamlet especially, who, in addition, asks to hear of the Trojan war from the Players, and reports his share in a sea-battle with pirates. . . .

A martial bearing in life, "An eye like Mars, to threaten and command", and martial honours in death are the marks of nobility, and it is appropriate that Hamlet's body should be carried off ceremoniously:

> Let four captains
> Bear Hamlet, like a soldier, to the stage. . .
> The soldiers' music and the rites of war
> Speak loudly for him.

(V, ii, 406–11)

There are other courtly accomplishments; one is the bookishness of Hamlet and the "scholar" Horatio, which links with the many classical references, and with the appreciation of the actors and their plays by Polonius and Hamlet; the latter's advice to the players may stem from the "saws of books" that "youth and observation" have copied in his mind. Books twice play some part in the action, first when Hamlet enters reading, to be disturbed by the questions of Polonius, and later when Ophelia pretends to be reading while waiting for him. . . .

Significant, too, is the strong religious emphasis in the play for its part in establishing the grace and ceremony of Elsinore, and the main impression is of dignity, pomp and pompousness, so that Laertes' complaint that his father has been given an obscure funeral stirs sympathy; it is wrong that such a high official and dignitary should receive

> No trophy, sword, nor hatchment o'er his bones,
> No noble rite nor formal ostentation.

(IV, v, 214–15)

ELSINORE A PRISON?

For all its spaciousness in diction, the court of Elsinore is closed and secretive. Only rarely does the action move into the open air; and in these scenes there is no sense of unoppressed space as on the wind-swept heath in *King Lear,* and no change of location, such as *Othello* shows with its transition from Venice to Cyprus, and *Macbeth* with its excursion into England. *Hamlet* is unusual among Shakespeare's plays, and unique among the tragedies, in maintaining a rough unity of place: the court is the focus of all the action, and no characters truly escape from it. Denmark, or more strictly Elsinore, is indeed a prison, as Hamlet says; he is not allowed to return to Wittenberg, and suffers restraint in more ways than one. When eventually he does leave the court, he goes under the close guard of Rosencrantz and Guildenstern and, if the intentions of Claudius were to be carried out, would be journeying to his death. On the way to England he is taken prisoner, ironically, by pirates, who treat him with more respect than did the king. The only other character of importance to depart the court is Laertes, and Polonius sends Reynaldo to spy on him in Paris. The Ghost comes from prison to warn Hamlet, from where he is "confined to fast in fires", and forbidden "to tell the secrets of my prison-house". . . .

In addition, Hamlet is under constant watch, spied on by Claudius and his agents Rosencrantz, Guildenstern, Polonius, and even by Ophelia, who is employed as a decoy in the nunnery scene; and in turn Hamlet and Horatio spy on Claudius in the play-scene. From the opening scene, with its group of characters keeping "this same strict and most observant watch", spying is one of the main characteristics of *Hamlet.* . . .

But what is seen has to be interpreted, and may still not reveal the truth; it may indeed be a deliberate attempt to mislead. Polonius reaches the wrong conclusions in spite of his zeal in looking into Ophelia's love for Hamlet. . . .

In his plans to murder Hamlet, Claudius tries to ensure that his stratagem will not be detected, that what is seen will be misinterpreted; but although he takes care to avoid trouble . . . his plans fail. Hamlet continually endeavours to see reality, and strip off false appearances; he employs the actors who "hold the mirror up to nature" to reveal what really happened at the death of his father, and . . . sets up a glass where Gertrude may "see the inmost part" of herself, and cries, showing her the two portraits of his father and Claudius,

> Have you eyes?
> Could you on this fair mountain leave to feed,
> And batten on this moor? Ha! have you eyes? . . .
>
> (III, iv, 65–7)

Polonius is killed while spying and Ophelia is spurned because she acts as a decoy; perhaps they would both have done better to follow Hamlet's advice, "Let the doors be shut upon him, that he may play the fool no where but in's own house". . . . In the last scene, when Hamlet recognizes treachery, he cries, "Ho! let the doors be lock'd", and the stage becomes a prison indeed for the final slaughter. . . .

For, as is continually brought out in action and image, the court of Elsinore is a prison, a place of spying and watching. All the characters must try to deceive each other, and in particular Hamlet and Claudius must conceal their true motives and aims. To do this, all indulge in play acting, make use of the artificial ceremonious court diction. . . .

"WE ARE ARRANT KNAVES ALL"

The court of Elsinore is then at the same time a place of nobility, chivalry, dignity, religion, and a prison, a place of treachery, spying and, underlying this, corruption. Both of these aspects are equally real and important. In the creation of both the play-scene is central, as it is central in time and action. Its dialogue of stiff rhymed couplets is the most formal and stately in the play, with its continual generalization:

> But what we do determine oft we break.
> Purpose is but the slave to memory. . . .
> The great man down, you mark his favourite flies;
> The poor advanced makes friends of enemies.
> And hitherto doth love on fortune tend;
> For who not needs shall never lack a friend,
> And who in want a hollow friend doth try,
> Directly seasons him his enemy. . . .
>
> (III, ii, 197 ff.)

The player's speeches, with their suggestion of an old-fashioned, stilted style, are only an extension of the stilted courtly diction, which occasionally suggests parallels with the diction of much earlier plays. . . .

Yet this formality embodies or is connected with all the good values of the court; the destruction of it is the destruction of something good, of the dignified courage with which Claudius outfaces the Danish rabble, of those qualities which go to make Horatio. . . .

These conflicting aspects of *Hamlet*, formality and corruption, point to an interpretation of the play. Hamlet has to fight continually to see what lies behind appearances, behind the court formality, in order to find out the truth about his father's death. Everywhere he finds or thinks he finds corruption of some kind behind the formal grace, so that he mistrusts the court diction and all the good values with which it is associated. When he turns on Ophelia,

Ophelia.   . . . their perfume lost,
          Take these again; for to the noble mind
          Rich gifts wax poor when givers prove unkind.
          There, my lord.
Hamlet.   Ha, ha! are you honest? . . .

                                                    (III, i, 99–103)

she addresses him with the aphoristic speech characteristic
of her father, and that in itself is enough to arouse his suspicion and hostility. Soon only the blunt Horatio, more an antique Roman than a Dane, the one character lacking in sub-
terfuge, remains faithful to him. Perhaps the most terrible
feature of his recognition of corruption everywhere is his
recognition of it in himself too; where others deceive he
must deceive too, where others act he must put on an antic
disposition, where the inmost desires and passions of others
must be revealed, so must his own passions be roused. And
where there is no legal punishment for his father's death, he
must stoop, driven by the universal wrong, and "being thus
be-netted round with villanies", to revenge. He must share
the corruption of others in spite of his nobility, and recognize in himself the common features, "We are arrant knaves
all". In this perhaps lies a clue to the tragedy, that in revealing the evil in others, Hamlet arouses evil passions in himself; that however clear the evidence may seem, the truth
may still escape.

Soliloquies and Other Wordplay Let the Audience Share Some of Hamlet's Thoughts

John Russell Brown

Shakespeare's characters often speak soliloquies, or speeches recited to themselves, to reveal their inner thoughts and feelings. Shakespeare also employed asides, usually single lines meant to be heard by the audience rather than the characters onstage, to achieve the same effect. John Russell Brown, distinguished first head of the Department of Drama and Theater Arts at the University of Birmingham and associate director of England's Royal National Theater, here explores Shakespeare's use of such wordplay in *Hamlet*. Besides soliloquies and asides, says Brown, the main character sometimes utters ambiguous, puzzling lines that no other characters understand. Sometimes the audience understands these lines, but other times it does not. Brown cites the example of a famous line from the Gravedigger's scene. Despite the fact that the audience is frequently privy to Hamlet's thoughts, Brown points out, Shakespeare wisely left a considerable amount to the spectators' imaginations. This invariably leaves them, at the end of a performance, slightly dissatisfied but strongly fascinated.

As Shakespeare wrote he seems to have been constantly aware of the audience's potential for interplay, and used soliloquies as the most positive way to set this going, and to direct it. . . . Characters and more are established in the audience's mind by means of soliloquies which invite the audience into the workings of their minds by an act of its own imagination. An interplay is set up which seems to put the audience in possession, so that later it will follow these characters at times when they speak no words at all. . . . Shakespeare came to trust his ability to arouse the audience's imaginations, so that it was in their minds that his plays became fully alive. Shakespeare was not only creative in himself, but the cause of creativity in others. Soliloquies were only one in a wide range of devices which he used to ensure the free and imaginative engagement of an audience.

THE AUDIENCE DRAWN INTO HAMLET'S PREDICAMENT

The first scene of *Hamlet* begins with an interchange between soldiers and Horatio, in which all are straining to see and then to understand the Ghost, so that by the second scene, when the prince is one member 'among others' at the court of King Claudius and his mother, the audience is prepared to search out the 'young Hamlet'. At first, however, it hears only bitter, tantalising wordplay from him:

> KING   But now, my cousin Hamlet, and my son—
> HAMLET   A little more than kin, and less than kind.
> KING   How is it that the clouds still hang on you?
> HAMLET   Not so, my lord; I am too much in the sun.
>
>   (I.ii.64–7)

Perhaps Hamlet's first line is spoken aside, to himself or to the audience, but it could be spoken without restraint to the king his uncle. In any of these ways, it would baffle full understanding of what Hamlet is trying to say or do, and break the previous interchange between characters. Here Shakespeare seems to challenge the audience to guess or to imagine what is that 'within which passes show' (l. 85). Then comes the soliloquy with which Hamlet is more fully presented and, in its harsh transitions, repetitions, progressive imagery, questioning—'Must I remember?'—and in its sudden stoppages, which are like seizures, his very being seems to lie open to the audience's apprehension. The soliloquy stops finally, when Hamlet addresses his 'heart' and not the audience: he may have heard Horatio and others entering or, perhaps, he is so aware of his own helplessness that he allows his thoughts to go no further:

> It is not, nor it cannot come to good.
> But break, my heart, for I must hold my tongue.
>
>   (ll. 158–9)

By any reckoning Hamlet is one of the most complex of Shakespeare's characters, and a series of soliloquies is only one of the means which encourage the audience to enter imaginatively into his very personal and frightening predicament. The play's narrative is handled so that a prolonged two-way chase is sustained between him and the king, during which the audience knows more than either one of them and so thinks ahead and anticipates events. In interplay with Rosencrantz, Guildenstern and Polonius, and perhaps with Claudius, Gertrude and Ophelia, Hamlet has asides to draw attention to what dialogue cannot express. At the performance of *The Mousetrap*, the play with which Hamlet hopes to 'catch the conscience of the king', his outspoken gibes while sitting with Ophelia ensure that the audience is alerted to watch Hamlet as much as either the play or the king. Yet here it cannot be in full possession of what he thinks; its imagination must either fasten on what can be held in the mind from among his savage, jocular wordplay or, failing to understand his words, sense only that some unspoken need or unprecedented pain is now at work. By this time in the play, a complex web of interactions is pulling the audience's attention in many ways, testing and widening its imaginative involvement.

SPEECHES THAT BAFFLE EVERYONE

When Hamlet returns after his journey to England, in Act V of the play, he has no more soliloquies of any length. In apparently casual manner, his thoughts are drawn out by the Gravedigger (who had started to dig graves the day Hamlet was born), by Laertes mourning Ophelia's corpse, and by the king. But on the other hand, his mother seems only to silence him. Now Shakespeare appears to be placing obstacles in the way of the audience's understanding of Hamlet's deepest, self-driven consciousness. Perhaps he speaks for himself, as if in soliloquy, as he is about to leave the stage near the close of the first of the two scenes:

> Let Hercules himself do what he may,
> The cat will mew, and dog will have his day.
>
> (ll. 285–6)

This couplet will taunt anyone seeking full understanding; the king cannot respond, beyond 'I pray thee, good Horatio, wait upon him', and the audience is placed in much the same position, however much it craves to know more.

At the start of the last scene, Hamlet seems to be offering a full and open account of himself to Horatio. But his friend's lame responses together with the pressure of events which is made apparent in Hamlet's own exclamations, needless repetitions and emphasis, imagery, and occasional withdrawals from explanation, continue to awaken the audience's sense that all is not yet capable of immediate comprehension. Then Osric . . . draws out other responses. Hamlet's readiness to spar with Osric using his own weapons of conceited speech may amaze the audience, as it does Horatio, even as laughter tends to take over. When Osric has gone, Hamlet's explanatory speech is equally baffling, voicing a concern with the 'state of Denmark' that has not been heard so clearly since he was called to witness the ghost. . . .

> 'A did comply, sir, with his dug [vulgar term for a nipple] before 'a suck'd it. Thus has he, and many more of the same bevy, that I know the drossy [scum-covered] age dotes on, only got the tune of the time and outward habit of encounter—a kind of yesty [bubbly or frothy] collection, which carries them through and through the most fann'd and winnowed opinions; and do but blow them to their trial, the bubbles are out.
>
> (V.ii.181–8)

Somewhere here, among repetitions and strange imagery of dugs and dross, the audience may be able to feed its own ideas of the prince, the time, an outward habit of encounter, the oncoming trial. In turn, the Lord also awakens a strange response, because Hamlet then goes on to say that mankind lives and dies according to some providence that has thought for a sparrow, and that 'the end'—his end—will come almost of its own accord. Very simple words echo the Bible's trust in a beneficent and all-powerful God, a thought entirely new to Hamlet and one that seems to reduce his role to one of merely passive submission. The hero enters his final 'trial' still prompting the audience to remain open to new impressions.

HAMLET'S LAST WORDS

A set speech about his 'madness' to Laertes and the assembled company, interchanges about the fencing foils (not knowing Laertes' treachery, as the audience does), the shortest of addresses to his mother, some taunting of his opponent—'I pray you pass with your best violence' (l. 290)—the 'incensed' fighting, followed by a threefold killing of the king, with two poisons and a rapier's point, all draw the audience's attention strongly forward towards each succeeding event. There is little doubt of the play's effect on its audience here: all is caught up with *what* happens, rather that with *how* it is

AN ACTOR WORKS AT CONNECTING WITH HIS AUDIENCE

In this excerpt from Mary Z. Maher's Modern Hamlets and Their Soliloquies, *renowned actor Ben Kingsley, who played Hamlet on stage in 1975, tells how he took advantage of the soliloquies to establish, as he put it, a flow of "juices" between the character and the audience.*

They [the spectators] were so close they were almost hanging off my nose, and I thought that if we didn't allow ourselves to connect with them we would lose out. There was so much energy pouring in from the audience. It is like tennis. The ball goes out to them and they react and then the ball goes back to the actor. But it also includes them, the essence of the play moves through the actors like a flame, a blazing torch which is passed around. You had to hand it back to the audience, but very delicately. . . .

I had terrific contact with the audience. . . . With my eyes, I create who the audience is and what they are and where their reality is. They can come and go as the actor pleases in terms of the soliloquy. The actor has the power to conjure, by a wave of the hand.

Their [the audience's] function changes a great deal. So, it's difficult to call them friends because in the next soliloquy you might be railing against them. People who—people for whom, *for* whom I was unfolding a great secret [he says this with great emphasis]. But not WITH whom, FOR whom. Only *occasionally* I would hope that they would feel that it was WITH as well as FOR.

All of the soliloquies very much included the fact that the audience were there looking at me. None of them were in the abstract. It was like—when I spoke to *myself,* I spoke to the *audience.* They were my ears. I addressed myself to them in the way that one would address oneself to oneself in an argument. I never asked them what I should do.

I never made any demands on them, but I always let them share the questions that I was asking myself. I think it's very difficult—an audience can't respond. They can't help the play other than by listening. So rather than "what shall I do" [he says this leaning forward in an aggressive and pronounced way], it's more like "what shall I do" [he says this quietly but still to an audience]. It's a case of not begging for an answer but telling them that I was in a very difficult position and only I could find a way out. I often let them off the hook in the soliloquy by indicating, "You can't help me out, you know—this is up to me and I'll have to take care of it."

Mary Z. Maher, *Modern Hamlets and Their Soliloquies.* Iowa City: University of Iowa Press, 1992, pp. 71–72.

happening. Indeed the final deaths succeed each other so swiftly that the exact means of some of them may remain obscure to watchers in the theatre. Then comes a much slower passage, with the off-stage sound of Fortinbras's approach and Hamlet struggling to speak. Yet even now Shakespeare arranged, very specifically, that Hamlet should not 'tell all', as once he had said an actor should:

> You that look pale and tremble at this chance,
> That are but mutes or audience to this act,
> Had I but time, as this fell sergeant Death
> Is strict in his arrest, O, I could tell you—
> But let it be.

(ll. 326–30)

The last words that Hamlet is given are the puzzling 'The rest is silence' (l. 350): the audience must rely on its own imaginations to sense whether this is spoken in despair or satisfaction. Does he want to say more and cannot, or does he long for the 'quietus' that is death? Do these words express a sudden horror as he faces death? The actor will guide the audience in one direction or another, but the context of this speech ensures and enhances the verbal ambiguity. Does Hamlet have to struggle to get his words out? . . . To whom are his last words addressed? They could be, like a soliloquy, spoken for himself or to the theatre audience; they could be spoken to those assembled on stage, explaining that he is unable to say more; or to his friend Horatio, in an attempt to console him. The ambiguous words may continue to disturb the audience while Horatio follows them, in a quite different vein, with pious consolation and a prayer that angels should sing Hamlet to a comfortable 'rest'. Then the audience is given yet another prompt to make its own responses when Fortinbras orders military honours for a prince who has not been 'put on' to a fair trial.

CHAPTER 2

The Play's Pivotal Characters

READINGS ON
HAMLET

Hamlet: A Man Who Thinks Before He Acts

Louis B. Wright and Virginia A. LaMar

Untold thousands of pages have been written about Hamlet's character and the so-called "Hamlet problem," consisting of the major questions about his motivations and behavior. Scholars and actors have attempted to answer these questions in numerous and diverse ways. In this concise essay, noted Shakespearean experts Louis B. Wright and Virginia A. LaMar of the Folger Shakespeare Library discuss the Hamlet problem, concentrating mostly on Hamlet's delay in enacting his revenge. They suggest that this delay is the result of the character's intellect and education, since both have trained him to reason things out rather than to act rashly, without thinking.

Much of the vast literature on this play has concentrated on the interpretation of Hamlet's character, particularly in attempting to explain his inability to take decisive action, his treatment of Ophelia, his madness, real or feigned, and a host of other questions called up by his actions. These constitute the "Hamlet problem." The answer is to be found in the study of Shakespeare's play as a piece for the public stage at the end of the sixteenth century rather than in subjecting Hamlet himself to psychoanalysis. Actually, Shakespeare's audience was not aware of a "Hamlet problem," and nobody for more than a century and a half worried about possible faults in Hamlet's character that made him put off killing Claudius. When someone finally raised the question of Hamlet's delay, an eighteenth-century critic, Thomas Hanmer, remarked that if the Prince had gone "naturally to work" in the first act, the play would have ended right there. When Shakespeare's audience went to the Globe in 1600, they expected to see a rousing melodrama in the popular

Reprinted, with minor editing, with the permission of Pocket Books, a division of Simon & Schuster, from *The Tragedy of Hamlet, Prince of Denmark* (The Folger Library General Reader's Shakespeare), by William Shakespeare, edited by Louis B. Wright and Virginia A. LaMar. Copyright © 1958 by Pocket Books.

genre of the revenge tragedy, and that is precisely what Shakespeare set out to give them, a play full of all the conventional trappings that audiences had learned to expect, including a great deal of suspense until the violent denouement [final outcome] of the last act. If *Hamlet* transcends the run-of-the-mill revenge play, that again is further proof of its author's genius; but one should always remember that Shakespeare was a practical man with an extraordinary sense of what is "good theatre" and that he always wrote with both eyes on the box office and never a glance toward posterity in Academia [the realm of scholarly research and analysis], a destiny that would have appalled him.

THREE-DIMENSIONAL CHARACTERS

Because *Hamlet* is a well-made revenge play designed to appeal to the taste of an Elizabethan audience that had whetted its appetite on the sensations served up in Thomas Kyd's *Spanish Tragedy*, Shakespeare's own *Titus Andronicus*, and an earlier but now lost *Tragedy of Hamlet*, it does not follow that it lacked the qualities of greatness. The most enduring plays have always been those that made a popular appeal in the theatre. "Intellectual" closet dramas have remained just there—in the closet. Shakespeare in *Hamlet* shows an understanding of human life and character that had deepened with his own maturity, and he expressed that knowledge in poetry that has become a part of the world's heritage of great literature. Proof of the permanent literary value of the play lies in its popularity as a work to be read. Thousands of persons who have never had an opportunity to see it on the stage have read it with pleasure and profit.

Much of the delight of modern readers, of course, comes from the study of the characters of the principal figures in the play, for Shakespeare has presented them in three-dimensional vividness. We feel that they are living beings with problems that are perennially human. If a modern man is not called upon, as Hamlet was, to avenge a murdered father, he nevertheless must face crises in his own life that remind him of Hamlet's dilemma, and he recognizes in the mental attitudes of the various persons of the play attitudes that are familiar in everyday life. Everybody has encountered an Ophelia, a sweet but uninspiring girl dominated by her father and brother. And everybody has had to put up with a Polonius, full of conceit over his worldly wisdom and ever ready to advise us with an unctuous cliché.

A Capable, Educated Prince

Inevitably, the modern reader's interest concentrates on the character of Hamlet himself. The play, after all, is about his problems, and the unusual care that Shakespeare took in writing his lines shows his own concern with the interpre-

Hamlet as a Player-Fool

In this excerpt from his book, The Masks of Hamlet, *Marvin Rosenberg of the University of California at Berkeley explains why he thinks the roles of "actor" and "jester" are important facets of Hamlet's character.*

Hamlet has another role that seems inborn: he is an actor, to theatre born. Later aspects of the role will be forced upon him: but even at the beginning we will want to sense the histrionic [play-acting] impulse that influences the way he may present himself to achieve an effect on others—and, when alone, on himself. He acts—putting on a mask that hides his own self, for strategy, for safety, counterattack, or a kind of enjoyment—always with the sense of an artist who cares about his art. "What a pity [Hamlet] was born to the throne,". . . [a noted Shakespearean critic] wrote in 1859, "he would have made his fortune on the stage.". . . We may imagine the plays Hamlet happily engaged in, as director-actor, in the palace and perhaps at early school and at Wittenberg. Certainly Hamlet is the only one of the major tragic heroes with a persistent sense of playfulness and humor. Even in his first scene a slight, grim touch of the Fool enters, as in his puns to Claudius, his jesting with Horatio—enough so we can recognize in ourselves as Hamlet the impulse to make fun, and make fun of, however oppressed by mourning, or unidentified miseries.

Hamlet, against as he is to seeming, is an accomplished seemer. There will be some times when Hamlet knows he is acting, we as Hamlet will know it, and the audience will know it. But there are other times we may not be able to recognize if he is (if we are) "on," or how much of what he does (we do) is acting. There is a subtle ambiguity here: when is Hamlet in fact deadly serious, furiously angry, hurting, and hurtful? How much of the self is at work, how much the role, how much the mask? This is one of the great mysteries of Hamlet's—and the human—condition: we all may be playing roles more than we can know. But when Hamlet doesn't know, will the actor (we) do his (our) best to let the audience know that he doesn't know?

Marvin Rosenberg, *The Masks of Hamlet.* Newark: University of Delaware Press, 1992, pp. 176–77.

tation of that part. We may be sure, however, that Shakespeare never intended to present Hamlet as a delicate
flower, too intellectual and sensitive to cope with the rude
milieu of the Danish court—an interpretation that Romantic
critics of the nineteenth century sometimes favored. Hamlet
was no Bunthone [a mild-mannered poet in Gilbert and Sul-
livan's operetta, *Patience*] and would not have "walked down
Piccadilly with a lily in his hand." On the contrary, Hamlet
reflected in his character qualities that an Englishman in
1600 would have understood as those to be expected in a
prince who had been educated to rule his country. From
what others say of him in the course of the action, we know
that Hamlet's melancholic attitude when the play opens is
not normal for him and that he was not characteristically in-
effectual in action. At his best, he possessed qualities and
abilities typical of the Renaissance ideal of the gentleman:
courage, generosity, learning, wit, courtly bearing, skill with
the sword, and a taste for music and drama. Only since his
father's death has he succumbed to melancholy which has
temporarily made him apathetic and slow to act.

DECISIONS BASED ON REASON

In discussing the meaning of *Hamlet* in Elizabethan terms,
Miss Lily Bess Campbell in *Shakespeare's Tragic Heroes*
shows with much plausibility that Shakespeare is intent
upon studying the effects of grief, not only upon Hamlet but,
with contrasting effect, upon Laertes and Fortinbras, who
suffer analogous losses. She demonstrates from contemporary evidence the notion that inconsolable grief such as
Hamlet experienced after the shock of his father's death left
the victim lethargic and inactive. But there is more to Shakespeare's treatment than this. The play and the characteriza-
tions are both complex, and the very complexity has proved
one of its fascinations for readers who like to dissect the personalities of the characters involved.

Hamlet, possessed of a finely trained intellect, is a man
with a philosophic approach to life. He has been at the University of Wittenberg, where he has engaged in the subtleties
of intellectual speculation. By training, such a man learns to
analyze problems, and his responses are never automatic
because his decisions come after contemplation rather than
from impulse. Though he may be slow to make a decision,
that decision will be based on reason.

Shakespeare's age was fond of debating the relative merits of the contemplative versus the active life. The ideal of education was a proper balance between the two, and the ideal courtier ... demonstrated both aspects. By implication, and by the words of other characters, Shakespeare gives Hamlet qualities familiar in the best of the Renaissance Englishmen. Though he did not neglect the active life, he found his greatest pleasure in the cultivation of his mind. Such a man, brought back to the sordid realities of the Danish court, might well complain against the cursed spite of fate that forced him to set right the evils around him. Complain though he might, he would not neglect his duty. Instead, he would study the problems before him and attempt their solution when he had satisfied his reason. If Hamlet's methods of working out his problems are indirect and time-consuming, he is merely following the pattern of behavior of the thoughtful and speculative type of thinker.

HAMLET'S PHILOSOPHIC MIND

A part of Hamlet's agony results from the very fact that he has a keen and alert mind that sees the implication of any potential action. When he finds Claudius at his prayers, he does not take his revenge by stabbing him but delays for a more fitting time. Had he reacted automatically, as the choleric Laertes would have done, he would have killed Claudius and realized too late that he had slain him in a moment of repentance and given him the rewards of heaven. The killing of Claudius would be an act of finality, but Hamlet, with his idealism so wounded by his knowledge of the evil surrounding him, was inhibited by his awareness that Claudius' death would not restore his own faith in the innate goodness of human life.

· Hamlet's qualities may be seen in many intellectual figures who enter public life and are brought face to face with the realities of practical politics. The happy politician is one who, unhampered by a philosophic mind, can respond automatically in accordance with the required conventions of behavior. The speculative thinker finds it difficult to react instantly and decisively in political crises. Perhaps one reason for the popularity of Hamlet is the sympathy which all thoughtful and studious persons must feel for the Prince, and their self-identification with his type.

The Ghost: Messenger from a Higher Court of Values?

Philip Edwards

Although the ghost of Hamlet's father has few lines in the play, the apparition on the battlements is one of the most crucial characters. The ghost is both the focal point of the betrayal and murder that brought about Claudius's accession to the throne and the instigator of Hamlet's quest for revenge. This essay is by Philip Edwards, a professor of English literature at the University of Liverpool and a leading Shakespearean commentator. In it, Edwards begins by describing the ghost's first appearance and its three commands it demands of Hamlet. More important than what the ghost says, however, Edward maintains, is its strange silence later, when the plot thickens and many people die. He goes on to explain how the ghost in this play differs markedly from the one in Kyd's *Spanish Tragedy*, the most famous revenge play before *Hamlet* was written. Edwards concludes with the suggestion that, in *Hamlet*, the ghost's silence leaves the audience, like the main character, wondering if the apparition was indeed real or merely part of the tortured prince's imagination. Is, then, the seeking of bloody vengeance sanctioned by the morality and justice of a higher, heavenly court?

Hamlet is galvanised into activity by the news of the appearance of a ghost that resembles his dead father. On the platform that night he sees it and is determined to speak to it whatever happens. It is explanation he wants; explanation and a course of action. 'Let me not burst in ignorance', he cries. 'What should we do?' Though it is specific explanation—why the Ghost has come—and a specific course of action—what the Ghost wants him to do—that he seeks, his words have a wider perspective. The Ghost may have some secret, some unimaginable truth to bring relief from those 'thoughts beyond the reaches of our souls', an explanation why things are as they are and a directive for meaningful action. To his demands in both their specific and their general senses he receives, or thinks he receives, a more than sufficient response.

THE GHOST'S THREE COMMANDS

The Ghost declares that he is his father's spirit, gives him the extraordinary tidings of murder and adultery, and asks him to take revenge. His injunctions are summed up in the three imperatives, 'Bear it not', 'Taint not thy mind', 'Leave her to heaven.' These interconnect. 'Bear it not' looks both backwards and forwards. The idea of retribution is implied by the Ghost's appeal to Hamlet's 'nature', that is, his filial piety. 'Bear it not' means that as a son he is not to acquiesce in and accept what has been done to his father. But it looks also to the future. The abuse of Denmark by the very continuation of this pair in sovereignty and in marriage is not to be endured: 'Bear it not.' The second imperative is very strange: 'howsomever thou pursues this act, / Taint not thy mind'. Whatever the exact meaning of 'taint', the tone of the remark is that the Ghost does not consider this matter of revenge too difficult an act, and is anxious that Hamlet should not become too disturbed about it. No doubt for the Ghost the challenge is like that which he accepted all those years ago when he agreed to face old Fortinbras in a single combat: a matter of honour, determination, courage and skill. The final injunction, 'Leave her to heaven', must temper our feeling of the Ghost's personal vindictiveness. It is more important, however, in giving a religious context to the punishment of Claudius and Gertrude. Gertrude's earthly punishment is to be her conscience: 'those thorns that in her bosom lodge / To prick and sting her'. Whatever further punishment or exoneration is hers to receive belongs to an after-life. With Claudius it is different. By his words 'Leave *her* to heaven', the Ghost must imply that a higher justice requires the exemplary punishment of Claudius on earth, by the hand of an appointed human being. The Ghost's commands indicate not the pursuit of personal satisfaction but the existence of a world beyond the human world responsible for justice in the human world. Whether the Ghost has the authority to convey this the play never makes clear.

Awful though it is, Hamlet now has his explanation. What had seemed the degeneration of the world turns out to be a condition which is clearly and starkly the consequence of a double crime. He now also has his directive, a commission that is also a mission. His reaction to the Ghost is like a religious conversion. He wipes away all previous knowledge, all previous values, and baptises himself as a new man (I.5.95–104).

> And thy commandment all alone shall live
> Within the book and volume of my brain,
> Unmixed with baser matter.

The commandment is summed up by the Ghost as 'Remember!' 'Remember me', says the Ghost, and Hamlet repeats the word three times in his dedication. The Ghost is to be remembered 'whiles memory holds a seat / In this distracted globe', that is to say so long as this now-disordered world attributes any value to the past and its traditions, to the established standards of virtue and justice. In this speech, to remember means more than to keep in mind; it means to maintain and to restore. . . . It is quite clear that Hamlet is not prepared to accept the 'It was' of time, and that he regards revenge as a task of creative remembrance, that is, the restoration of a society that has fallen to pieces. The act ends with

> The time is out of joint: O cursed spite,
> That ever I was born to set it right.

This is a terrible moment as, all exhilaration gone, he faces the burden of his responsibilities. But who has told him that it is his responsibility to put the world to rights? to restore the disjointed frame of things to its true shape? No one but himself. It is the entirely self-imposed burden of cleansing the world that he now groans under. . . .

GUIDED BY HEAVEN?

What does the Ghost think of [Hamlet's final achievement of revenge and the many deaths accompanying it?]. . . . He has disappeared. There is no word of approval, or sorrow, or anger. He neither praises his dead son nor blames him. Nor, if he was a devil, does he come back to gloat over the devastation he has caused. The rest is silence indeed.

In Kyd's *Spanish Tragedy*, the ghost of the dead Andrea and his escort from the infernal world of spirits, named Revenge, were on stage during the whole of the play. It was ab-

solutely clear that the ultimate direction of things was entirely in the hands of the gods of the underworld. At the end
of the play Andrea rejoiced in the fulfilment of his revenge
and happily surveyed the carnage on the stage. 'Ay, these
were spectacles to please my soul!' He helped to apportion
eternal sentences, whose 'justice' makes our blood run cold.

In spite of the seeming crudity of *The Spanish Tragedy*, it
is a subtle and sinister view of the relation of gods and men
that the play conveys. Kyd's gods are dark gods. Men and
women plot and scheme to fulfil their desires and satisfy
their hatreds, they appeal to heaven for guidance, help and
approval, but the dark gods are in charge of everything, and
they use every morsel of human striving in order to achieve
their predestined purposes. Hieronimo's heroic efforts to obtain justice, which drive him into madness and his wife to
suicide, are nothing to the gods except as they may be used
to fulfil their promise to Andrea.

Hamlet resists the grim certainties of Kyd's theology and
the certainties of any other. . . . Hamlet is a tragic hero who at
a time of complete despair hears a mysterious voice uttering
a directive which he interprets as a mission to renovate the
world by an act of purifying violence. But this voice is indeed
a questionable voice. How far it is the voice of heaven, how its
words are to be translated into human deeds, how far the will
of man *can* change the course of the world—these are questions that torment the idealist as he continues to plague the
decadent inhabitants, as he sees them, of the Danish court.

His doubts, at one edge of his nature, are as extreme as his
confidence at the other. His sense of his freedom to create
his own priorities and decisions, and indeed his sense of
being heaven's scourge and minister privileged to destroy at
will, bring him to the disaster of killing Polonius, from
which point all changes, and he becomes the hunted as well
as the hunter. Eventually, in a new humility as his 'deep
plots' pall, Hamlet becomes convinced that heaven is guid-
ing him and that the removal of Claudius is a task that he is
to perform at the peril of his immortal soul. He does indeed
kill Claudius, but the cost is dreadful. What has he achieved,
as he dies with Claudius?

LIKE WE DO, HAMLET DOUBTED GHOSTS

It is very hard for us in the twentieth century to sympathise
with Hamlet and his mission. Hearing voices from a higher

world belongs mainly in the realm of abnormal psychology. Revenge may be common but is hardly supportable. The idea of purifying violence belongs to terrorist groups. Gertrude's sexual behaviour and remarriage do not seem out of the ordinary. Yet if we feel that twentieth-century doubt hampers our understanding of the seventeenth-century *Hamlet*, we must remember that *Hamlet* was actually written in our own age of doubt and revaluation—only a little nearer its beginning. *Hamlet* takes for granted that the ethics of revenge are questionable, that ghosts are questionable, that the distinctions of society are questionable, and that the will of heaven is terribly obscure. The higher truth which Hamlet tries to make active in a fallen world belongs to a past which he sees slipping away from him. Shakespeare movingly presents the beauty of a past in which kingship, marriage and the order of society had or was believed to have a heavenly sanction. A brutal Cain-like murder destroys the order of the past. Hamlet struggles to restore the past, and as he does so we feel that the desirability is delicately and perilously balanced against the futility. . . . This matter of balance is an essential part of our answer about the ending of the play. It is a precarious balance, and perhaps impossible to maintain.

The Elizabethans too doubted ghosts. Shakespeare used the concern of his time about voices and visions to suggest the treacherousness of communication with the transcendent world. We come in the end to accept the Ghost not as a devil but as a spirit who speaks truth yet who cannot with any sufficiency or adequacy provide the answer to Hamlet's cry, 'What should we do?' Everything depends on interpretation and translation. A terrible weight of responsibility is thrown on to the human judgement and will. . . . These distinctions between acts of faith and the demoniacal, between holy works and works of man's imagination, seem fundamental to *Hamlet*. We know that Hamlet made a mess of what he was trying to do. The vital question is whether what he was trying to do was a holy work or a work of man's imagination. Shakespeare refuses to tell us.

Hamlet's attempt to make a higher truth operative in the world of Denmark, which is where all of us live, is a social and political disaster, and it pushes him into inhumanity and cruelty. But the unanswerable question, 'Is't not to be damned / To let this canker of our nature come / In further evil?', if it could be answered 'Yes!' would make us see the chance-medley of the play's ending in a light so different that it would abolish our merely moral judgement. [Noted Shakespearean scholar, A.C.] Bradley's final remark on the play was that 'the apparent failure of Hamlet's life is not the ultimate truth concerning him'. But it might be. That is where the tragic balance lies. The play of *Hamlet* takes place within the possibility that there is a higher court of values than those which operate around us, within the possibility of having some imperfect communication with that court, within the possibility than an act of violence can purify, within the possibility that the words 'salvation' and 'damnation' have meaning. To say that these possibilities are certainties is to wreck the play as surely as to say they are impossibilities.

So the silence of the Ghost at the end of the play leaves the extent of Hamlet's victory or triumph an open question. To answer it needs a knowledge that Horatio didn't have, that Shakespeare didn't have, that we don't have. The mortal havoc is plain to our eyes on the stage; the rest is silence.

Ophelia: Madness Her Only Safe Haven

Michael Pennington

Michael Pennington is a noted Shakespearean actor and scholar; and his having both acted in and written about *Hamlet* puts him in the unique position of viewing the play from two very different but complementary vantage points. In this excerpt from his informative book, *"Hamlet": A User's Guide*, he analyzes Ophelia's character. Pennington begins with a glimpse of the dysfunctional family relationships that marked her upbringing and then provides a stunning description of the symptoms of her madness.

The ambiguities in Polonius's family are vexing but extremely playable: the group is by turns attractive and slightly repellent. . . .

Polonius is a bad parent, no doubt about it, bringing the manners of his working life home with him, egotistical and untrusting as men alone with their children can be. He clearly doesn't listen to his daughter at all, and there is nowhere a single word of affection from him towards either her or Laertes. Even the small formal apology to Ophelia for having misread Hamlet sounds like regret for a professional mistake. The restraint that he might have felt as a father doesn't prevent him exposing Ophelia to the ordeal of the Nunnery Scene; and quite possibly it is Hamlet's awareness of this trick that makes him torment her. Polonius takes no step to protect or comfort her either then or after the Play Scene, but is immediately bustling about and intriguing once again. . . . His brusqueness might accord with a certain kind of dumb male love: perhaps . . . his over-solicitude to Ophelia masks real protectiveness. But Ophelia's obvious repression and Laertes's failings as a human being give the lie to any idea of family health. Both son and daughter seriously

Reprinted from *"Hamlet": A User's Guide* by Michael Pennington (New York: Limelight Editions, 1996), by permission of Proscenium Publishers. Copyright 1996 by Michael Pennington.

lose personality when their father is present, Laertes disappearing behind formalities and Ophelia losing her mischief. Meanwhile Laertes is not much good with Ophelia, mad or sane. Yet Polonius's death (together with Hamlet's rejection) is enough to send Ophelia mad. . . .

THE WOMAN SHE MIGHT HAVE BECOME

In the early stages, Ophelia is hardly there at all. With Polonius she seems almost offensively mute and compliant: 'I shall obey, my Lord. . . no, my good Lord, but as you did instruct. . . . I do not know, my Lord, what I should think', rising in protest only as far as

> My lord, he hath importun'd me with love
> In honourable fashion

—and in the Nunnery Scene she becomes bewildered to the point of stupidity. Only when Hamlet leaves her does she begin to wake up: her idealised description of him is interrupted by the sudden sound of sweet bells jangled; and from here on, as the character looks down her abyss, the part looks up. However, this startling image is not the first hint of a talent gasping in an airless household: her description of Hamlet's visit to her 'all unbrac'd' is famous because of the descriptive power she brings to it, and in her first scene she shows a brief sense of humour—and a delightful turn of phrase—with Laertes:

> Do not, as some ungracious pastors do,
> Show me the steep and thorny way to heaven
> Whilst like a puff'd and reckless libertine
> Himself the primrose path of dalliance treads. . .

She is not afraid of her brother—she understands him and tolerates his pompous advice with love:

> 'Tis in my memory lock'd
> And you yourself shall keep the key of it.

This is the woman she might have become—warm, tolerant and imaginative. Instead she becomes jagged, benighted and imaginative:

> They say the owl was a baker's daughter. Lord, we know what
> we are, but know not what we may be. God be at your table!

Ophelia is made mad not only by circumstance but by something in herself. A personality forced into such deep hiding that it has seemed almost vacant has all the time been so painfully open to impressions that they now usurp her re-

flexes and take possession of her. She has loved, or been prepared to love, the wrong man, her father has brought disaster on himself, and she has no mother: she is terribly lonely.
Her existence has been all restraints, and when they are removed, a secret life rises up and floods her.

UNACCEPTABLY SANE

Madness is the safest place for Ophelia: it is where she expresses herself. She may not be a particularly good singer,

---

ONE OF DESTINY'S CASUALTIES
Here, from her entertaining book, The Friendly Shakespeare, *scholar Norrie Epstein, like Pennington, stresses
that because of the way men use and abuse her Ophelia sadly
never learns "what she might have been."*

It is Ophelia, not Hamlet, who most commands our sympathy.
One of destiny's casualties, she's swept along by political events
just as she is borne by the river at her death. . . .
     At her first appearance we see an innocent, trusting, and spir-
ited young girl, but by her last scene she is contaminated, mad,
and knowing. Whatever she might have become has been
blighted. Insane, Ophelia at last speaks the truth, although no
one understands her, and Shakespeare gives her one of the most
cryptic lines in the play: "Lord, we know what we are, but know
not what we may be." Ophelia goes mad because she discovers
what others "may be." Tragically, she never learns what she
might have become. . . .
     After her lover has killed her father, Ophelia's mind snaps. The
stage direction of the mad scene in the First Quarto has her entering with "her hair downe," an Elizabethan shorthand for de-
mentia and grieving. During this time women wore their hair
tightly bound, a coiffure that serves as a metaphor for their social
and physical constraints. Thus, to "let your hair down" meant total liberation, and, to Shakespeare's audience, madness. Ophelia's
mind, molded and shaped by her father, her brother, and the
court, has at last burst free. The lewd ballads and ditties she
sings have puzzled critics and inspired varied interpretations of
her character: how could such a guileless maiden know of such
"country matters"? They have been imprinted there precisely by
those who sought to shield her from such knowledge. All the
secret filth that lies rotting in the heart of the Danish court rises
to the surface—within Ophelia's mind.

Norrie Epstein, *The Friendly Shakespeare: A Thoroughly Painless Guide to the Best of
the Bard.* New York: Viking Penguin, 1993, pp. 332–34.

but she responds to the sounds, voices and pictures jangling in her head. She remembers folk-songs she didn't know she knew. All the channels blocked by 'sanity' open wide, her skin becomes super-sensitive, her glands secrete. She can hear the passage of time like a synaesthetic [deeply-felt sensation]. She can read people's minds, and sees a grimacing villain when she looks at Claudius, and a nymphomaniac greed behind the Queen's sympathy. She knows somehow that Laertes is on his way to right her wrongs—in fact to reclaim her—and she addresses him momentarily as a lover. She calls everyone 'ladies'. She may be incontinent [unable to control herself]. Silence dins in her ears as loudly as the waters she will eventually sink into. She is knowing where she was innocent, astute where she was helpless, satirical where she was bland. In spite of her disorders, there is not a line she speaks which is not humming with meaning, warning and portent. She is not so much mad as unacceptably sane. Hamlet and Polonius and Laertes (by his absence) have ruined her life, and her spirit takes flight in a one-winged, raucous trajectory before dropping like a stone to the ground.

Her dominant theme is her father's death (in production, Ophelias very typically wear a garment of Polonius's, so he is back among us), but her imagery tangles him, Hamlet and even Laertes together in a brilliant psychological displacement. Hamlet appears in the scene as the young man in the Saint Valentine's Day song that tells of a virgin who comes to his window—he promises to wed her, and then rejects her exactly because she sleeps with him. In Ophelia's case it was the other way round—it was Hamlet who visited her chamber, partly naked—but the young man's dirty trick in the song matches the bleak cruelty of Hamlet's verbal games: 'I did love you once. . . I loved you not. . . get thee to a nunnery'.

HER FOOTHOLD IN THE WORLD LOST

Even the sturdiest intellects seem to come over a bit sentimental when it comes to Ophelia: this is because of the flowers. I think they should be real—though a list that includes fresh rue and columbines as well as rosemary, pansies, fennel and daisies is certainly a headache for a prop buyer [person who buys the objects needed for a stage show], and no doubt they will end up being made, making that unconvincing dry slap on the stage when dropped. But, apart from the pleasant incongruity of Laertes, Gertrude and especially Claudius having to hold the flowers Ophelia gives them, the truthfulness of their colour and texture and the girl's precise knowledge of them is very moving; they are beautiful things withered by the fetid air of Elsinore. Her understanding of them is sane and exact: I have seen Ophelias holding weeds and grasses and imagining them flowers, even holding nothing at all and doing the same thing—both these solutions draw attention to her derangement, which we know, and her imaginative gifts, which we also know. The reality is much more powerful.

At first blush, Ophelia is not a patch on [no match for] her predecessors [earlier female characters of Shakespeare's]— Juliet, Rosalind or even Anne Page—and less still on what followed: Viola, Perdita, Cordelia, Miranda. With the special exception of Viola . . . these women stand up to their fathers, and if necessary to their lovers. Ophelia, doing neither, describes the oddest arc [undergoes the oddest personality change], finally winning the right to say anything she likes to anyone, but at the cost of her foothold in the world. The last we see of her, she is being thrown about in a grave, just as she was thrown about in life: shouted over by two assertive young men vying with each other over who loved her more, when there is no great evidence that either of them did very much. Rest in peace.

Gertrude: Scheming Adulteress or Loving Mother?

Rebecca Smith

Gertrude, Hamlet's mother, is one of the most crucial characters in the play because she is the focus of the love and/or anger of the trio of men who have been or are in contention for Denmark's throne—Hamlet's father, Claudius, and Hamlet himself. As University of Northern Texas scholar Rebecca Smith explains in this comprehensive essay, most stage and film directors have portrayed Gertrude as a scheming, guilty person. Certainly, says Smith, in the earlier versions of the story—the original Danish chronicle, Belleforest's French version, and the lost play (the so-called *Ur-Hamlet*)—the Danish queen *is* shown as a guilty transgressor. However, Smith suggests, Shakespeare fleshed out the character and in so doing made her more sympathetic. In his timeless version, Gertrude is less aware of any wrongdoing. She is more of an innocent sex object manipulated by her husband and son and frustrated by her desire to love and please both of them.

Gertrude, in Shakespeare's *Hamlet,* has traditionally been played as a sensual, deceitful woman. Indeed, in a play in which the characters' words, speeches, acts, and motives have been examined and explained in myriad ways, the depiction of Gertrude has been remarkably consistent, as a woman in whom "compulsive ardure . . . actively doth burn, / And reason [panders] will" (III.iv. 86–88) Gertrude prompts violent physical and emotional reactions from the men in the play, and most stage and film directors . . . have simply taken the men's words and created a Gertrude based on their reactions. But the traditional depiction of Gertrude is a false one, because what *her* words and actions actually create is a soft, obedient, dependent, unimaginative woman who is caught miserably at the center of a desperate struggle between two "mighty opposites," her "heart cleft in twain" (III.iv.156) by divided loyalties to husband and son. She loves both Claudius and Hamlet, and their conflict leaves her bewildered and unhappy.

THE STANDARD VIEW OF GERTRUDE

Three famous film versions of *Hamlet* illustrate the standard presentation, wherein Gertrude is a vain, self-satisfied woman of strong physical and sexual appetites. Thus, [director] Grigori Kozintsev (1964) shows her gazing into a hand mirror and arranging her hair as she chastens Hamlet for the particularity of his grief in the face of the commonness of death. Tony Richardson (1969) repeatedly shows her eating and drinking. . . . Gertrude sustains herself throughout the play with frequent goblets of greedily swilled wine.

In the same way, in the Olivier *Hamlet* (1948), the dramatic symbol for Gertrude is a luxurious canopied bed. This bed is one of the first and last images on the screen and emphasizes both Gertrude's centrality in the play and Olivier's interpretation of the centrality of sexual appetite in Gertrude's nature. Even her relationship with her son is tinged with sexuality. Olivier's Hamlet brutally hurls Gertrude—the ultimate sexual object—onto her bed, alternating embraces and abuse in the accusatory closet scene. In Richardson's and Kozintsev's film versions, the sexual passion between Claudius and Gertrude receives similarly emphatic treatment. For example, Richardson has Claudius and Gertrude conduct much royal business from their bed; and in one particularly obvious scene, Kozintsev's Gertrude is led by Claudius through the midst of people scantily costumed as satyrs and nymphs and dancing in frenzied celebration. She is then literally pushed into a darkened room, whereupon Claudius moves toward her (and the camera) with a lustfully single-minded expression on his face. The misrepresentations that these film versions of Gertrude perpetuate . . . seem to assume that only a deceitful, highly sexual woman could arouse such strong responses and violent reactions in men, not a nurturant and loving one, as is Shakespeare's Gertrude.

THE EARLY VERSIONS OF THE CHARACTER

Gertrude, like Hamlet, is a character who undergoes subtle but significant changes between Shakespeare's sources and his play, changes which increase her complexity and ambiguity. In the earliest Amleth/Hamlet stories, Gertrude clearly is culpable. In Saxo Grammaticus's twelfth-century *Historiae Danicae*, Gerutha/Gertrude marries Feng/Claudius, who is the known murderer of her husband. François de Belleforest, in his sixteenth-century retelling of the story in the *Histoires Tragiques*, makes one important addition to the depiction of Gertrude: he states that the Queen committed adultery with her brother-in-law during her marriage to the King. Finally, in the *Ur-Hamlet*, significant actions by Gertrude reinforce the suspicion of her culpability: "After the death of Corambis (Polonius) she blames herself for Hamlet's madness, and believes that she is thereby punished for her incestuous re-marriage, or else that her marriage, by depriving Hamlet of the crown, has driven him mad from thwarted ambition. Hamlet upbraids her for her crocodile tears, and urges her to assist in his revenge, so that in the King's death her infamy should die." In this earlier version, Gertrude . . . sends Hamlet warnings by Horatio, thus taking direct steps to aid Hamlet's revenge and thereby rid herself of guilt. . . .

Shakespeare's play apparently follows the main lines of the *Ur-Hamlet* (with its secret murder, doubtable ghost, feigned and real madness, play-within-a-play, closet scene, killing of the Polonius/Corambis figure, voyage to England, suicide of Ophelia, and fencing match with Laertes—Shakespeare's additions including only the pirates, Fortinbras, and possibly the gravediggers). The changes that Shakespeare does make in the structure and characters of the play demand attention as significant indicators of a redirection that adds subtlety and thematic complexity. . . . In Shakespeare's *Hamlet*, many questions about Gertrude arise that cannot be fully answered: the murder of old Hamlet is not public knowledge, but does Gertrude know, or at least suspect? Is she guilty of past adultery as well as current incest? Does the closet scene demonstrate her acknowledgment of sexual guilt, and does she thereafter align herself with Hamlet in his quest for revenge and thus shun Claudius's touch and bed? Indeed, does Gertrude demonstrate change and development in the course of the play, or is she incapable of change?

THE GHOST'S OBSESSION WITH GERTRUDE

Finding answers to these questions about Gertrude is complicated by the fact that in *Hamlet* one hears a great deal of discussion of Gertrude's personality and actions by other characters. She is a stimulus for and object of violent emotional reactions in the ghost, Hamlet, and Claudius, all of whom offer extreme descriptions of her. The ghost expresses simultaneous outrage, disgust, and protectiveness in his first appearance to Hamlet: "Let not the royal bed of Denmark be / A couch for luxury and damned incest. / But howsomever thou pursues this act, / Taint not thy mind, nor let thy soul contrive / Against thy mother aught" (I.v.82–86). The ghost firsts asks Hamlet for revenge, describes his present purgatorial state, spends ten lines sketchily outlining the secret murder, and then begins a vivid sixteen-line attack on the sexual relationship of Claudius and Gertrude (42–57). He returns to a brief description of the actual murder only because he "scent[s] the morning air, / Brief let me be" (58–59). Before he disappears, he returns to the topic of Gertrude's sexual misdeeds, but again admonishes Hamlet to "leave her to heaven." The ghost's second appearance to Hamlet is prompted by the need for further defense of Gertrude. Hamlet's resolution when he is preparing to visit his mother's bedchamber . . . seems to be failing. His frenzied attack on Gertrude gains verbal force and violence (which, on stage, is usually accompanied by increasing physical force and violence) until the ghost intervenes. Hamlet shares the ghost's obsession with Gertrude's sexuality, but is dissipating the energy that should be directed toward avenging his father's murder in attacking Gertrude. . . . The ghost must intervene to . . . command Hamlet to protect Gertrude, to "step between her and her fighting soul.". . .

HAMLET'S AND CLAUDIUS'S OBSESSIONS WITH GERTRUDE

Hamlet's violent emotions toward his mother are obvious from his first soliloquy, in which twenty-three of the thirty-one lines express his anger and disgust at what he perceives to be Gertrude's weakness, insensitivity, and, most important, bestiality: "O most wicked speed: to post / With such dexterity to incestious [*sic*] sheets" (I.ii.156–57). . . .

Later, when the ghost tells Hamlet that Claudius, Gertrude's second husband, is the murderer of her first, his generalized outrage at women increases and spreads. His sense of betrayal is soon further fed by the unexpected rejection of his love by Ophelia, who obeys the commands of her brother and father that result from their one-dimensional conception of a woman as a sexual "object.". . . Hereafter, Hamlet is described by Ophelia as behaving quite strangely (II.i.74–97), and he is heard by the audience speaking to Ophelia abusively or coarsely, as he does to his mother. His experiences lead him to attack what he perceives to be the brevity of women's love (I.ii.129–59; III.ii.154), women's wantonness (III.i.145), and the ability that women have to make "monsters" of the men (III.i.138) over whom they have so much power. . . .

Claudius creates an impression of Gertrude for the audience because she is the object of violent conflicting emotions for him as she is for the ghost and Hamlet. She is, he says, "My virtue or my plague" (IV.vii.13). He suffers under a "heavy burthen" (III.i.53) of guilt, but he refuses to give up "those effects for which I did the murther: / My crown, mine own ambition, and my queen" (III.iii.54–55). He speaks respectfully to Gertrude throughout the play, and tells Laertes that one of the reasons for his toleration of Hamlet's extraordinary behavior is his love for Gertrude. . . .

In Belleforest's version of the Hamlet story, the Claudius figure kills the King ostensibly to save the life of the Queen, his mistress. In Shakespeare's *Hamlet*, Gertrude's attractiveness for Claudius is one of the causes—and his sexual possession of her one of the results—of the murder of old Hamlet. . . . Claudius is as obsessed by Gertrude as the two Hamlets are, and—although he clearly loves her—he shares the Hamlets' conception of Gertrude as an *object*. She is "possess'd" as one of the "effects" of his actions (III.iii.53–54) and is thereafter "Taken to wife (I.ii.14). It may then seem contradictory that he does not forcibly stop Gertrude from drinking the poisoned wine, but there are, in the context of the final scene of the play, many strong reasons for his self-restraint. . . .

GERTRUDE'S SPEECHES

Although she may have been partially responsible for Claudius's monstrous act of fratricide and although her marriage to Claudius may have been indirectly responsible for making a "monster" of Hamlet, Gertrude is never seen in the play inducing anyone to do anything at all monstrous. . . . When one closely examines Gertrude's actual speech and actions in an attempt to understand the character, one finds little that hints at hypocrisy, suppression, or uncontrolled passion and their implied complexity.

Gertrude appears in only ten of the twenty scenes that comprise the play; furthermore, she speaks very little, having less dialogue than any other major character in *Hamlet*—a mere 157 lines out of 4,042 (3.8 percent). She speaks plainly, directly, and chastely when she does speak, using few images except in the longest of her speeches, which refer to Hamlet's and Ophelia's relationship, to Ophelia's death, to her sense of unspecified guilt, and to Hamlet's madness in the graveyard. . . .

Gertrude's brief speeches include references to honor, virtue, flowers, and a dove's golden couplets; neither structure nor content suggests wantonness. Gertrude's only mildly critical comments are in response to the verbosity of Polonius ("More matter with less art"—II.ii.95) and that of the Player Queen ("The lady doth protest too much, methinks"—III.ii.230).

Gertrude usually asks questions (ten questions in her approximately forty-five lines of dialogue in the closet scene) or voices solicitude for the well-being and safety of other characters. She divides her concern between Claudius and Hamlet; indeed, Claudius observes that she "lives almost by his [Hamlet's] looks" (IV.vii.12). Her first speeches are to Hamlet, admonishing an end to his "particular" grief and pleading that he stay in Denmark with her. . . . In her second appearance on stage, she directs Rosencrantz and Guildenstern "to visit / My too much changed son" (II.ii.35–36) in an attempt to discover the cause of his change. . . .

NO PROOF OF HER GUILT

Gertrude's actions are as solicitous and unlascivious as her language. She usually enters a scene with the King, and she is alone on stage only with Hamlet in the closet scene and with mad Ophelia (both times expressing feelings of some kind of guilt). She repeatedly leaves scenes after being ordered out by Claudius, which he does both to protect her from the discovery of his guilt and to confer with her privately about how to deal with Hamlet. Little proof for the interpretation of

Gertrude as a guileful [crafty] and carnal woman emerges from her other textually implicit actions, as, for example, when she sorrowfully directs the attention of Polonius and Claudius to Hamlet: "But look where sadly the poor wretch comes reading" (II.ii.168). . . . She later sends messengers to Hamlet to bring him to her after "The Mousetrap" and attempts to deal roundly with him, but she is forced to sit down and to contrast the pictures of her first husband and Claudius (III.iv.34, 53). Even after her encounter with Hamlet in the closet scene, she apparently attempts to restrain Laertes physically when he madly bursts in to accuse Claudius of killing Polonius. . . . She accepts a sprig of rue from Ophelia, to be worn "with a difference" (IV.v.183), and later scatters flowers on Ophelia's grave. It also is observable from the text that she offers Hamlet a napkin with which to wipe his face during the fencing match and wipes his face for him once. Finally, and most important, she drinks the poisoned wine and dies onstage, using her dying words to warn Hamlet of the poison (v.ii.291, 309–10). . . .

Her own words and actions compel one to describe Gertrude as merely a quiet, biddable, careful mother and wife. Nonetheless, one can still examine Gertrude's limited actions and reactions to answer the knotty interpretative question of Gertrude's culpability [guilt] in the murder of her first husband. When speaking to Hamlet, the ghost does not state or suggest Gertrude's guilt in his murder, only in her "falling-off" from him to Claudius (I.v.47). When Hamlet confronts her after "The Mousetrap," she asks in apparent innocence, "What have I done, that thou dar'st wag thy tongue / In noise so rude against me?" (III.iv.39–40). She has not been verbally guileful before, so one has no reason to suspect her of duplicity in this instance. And when Hamlet informs her that old Hamlet was murdered by Claudius, she does not indicate prior knowledge. Instead, she exclaims in horror, "As kill a King!" (30), and pleads for the third time that Hamlet mitigate his attack: "No more!" (101). She is not aware of any personal guilt, and she does not want to hear of the guilty deeds of one of the men she loves. . . .

HER HEART "CLEFT IN TWAIN"

Gertrude does readily admit her one self-acknowledged source of guilt—that her marriage was "o'erhasty," but in all other instances she feels guilt only after Hamlet has insisted

that she be ashamed. And it is not ever completely clear to
what Gertrude refers in the closet scene when she mentions
the black spots on her soul—if it is a newly aroused awareness of her adulterate and incestuous relationship, if it is her
marriage to a man whom Hamlet so clearly despises, or if it is
merely her already lamented o'erhasty marriage:

> O Hamlet, speak no more!
> Thou turn'st my [eyes into my very] soul,
> And there I see such black and [grained] spots
> As will [not] leave their tinct.

> (III.iv.88–91)

Hamlet's violent cajolery in the closet scene has created un-
accustomed feelings of guilt in this accommodating woman,
who wants primarily to please him. However, she has not
pleased Hamlet by acting in a way that pleased Claudius—by
marrying him so soon after her husband's death. . . . For Hamlet, her act "roars so loud and thunders in the index"
(III.iv.52), and his displeasure has "cleft" the Queen's heart
"in twain" (156) because she obviously loves both Hamlet and
Claudius and feels pain and guilt at her inability to please
both. . . .

Since the beginning of the play, Hamlet has been obsessed
with Claudius's and Gertrude's guilt, and it is this which pre-
cipitates his distempered behavior. Indeed . . . Gertrude's behavior at "The Mousetrap" would lead no one to believe that
she has seen herself reflected in the Player Queen. However,
Hamlet believes that she has—and Hamlet is a powerful first-
person force in the play who encourages one to see all events
and people from his perspective, nearly compelling one to see
Gertrude's one-line response to the play's action as an admission of guilt: "The lady doth protest too much, methinks"
(III.ii.230). Gertrude's remark at this play-within-the-play can
be given another interpretation that may be more accurate, in
view of Gertrude's accommodating, dependent personality:
her words are not a guileful anticipation and deflection of
comparisons between herself and the Player Queen. Instead,
being a woman of so few words herself, Gertrude must sin-
cerely be irritated by the Player Queen's verbosity, just as she
was earlier by that of Polonius. Obviously, Gertrude believes
that quiet women best please men, and pleasing men is
Gertrude's main interest. Indeed, Gertrude's concern to maintain a strong relationship with two men is demonstrated by
her only other lines at the play—brief lines—asking her "dear

Hamlet" to sit beside her (108) and voicing distress for Claudius's obvious consternation at the end of the play: "How fares my lord?" (267). After the play, Gertrude is, according to Guildenstern, "in most great affliction of spirit.". . . In no way by word or act, does she indicate that the play has sponta-neously created any sense of guilt in her.

GERTRUDE A SEXUAL OBJECT

Obviously, this analysis of Gertrude's behavior does not sug-gest any changes or clear moral development in her. . . . That Gertrude does not promise Hamlet to refrain from going to Claudius's bed may possibly suggest an admission of guilt about the relationship. Those who claim that Gertrude does admit to committing adultery and incest cite her one self-revealing aside, four lines in which she directly grieves for her sinful, sick soul and self-destructive, fearful guilt:

> To my sick soul, as sin's true nature is,
> Each toy seems prologue to some great amiss,
> So full of artless jealousy is guilt,
> It spills itself in fearing to be spilt.

> (IV.v.17–20)

But the nature of this lamented guilt remains unclear; it is ap-parently unfelt until aroused by Hamlet's attack. If it arises out of the conflict between her love for Claudius and her remorse for betraying the memory of her first husband, she obviously chooses, like Claudius, to "retain th'offense" (III.iii.56), be-cause she soon thereafter tries physically and verbally to pro-tect Claudius from Laertes.

Gertrude has not moved in the play toward independence or a heightened moral stance; only her divided loyalties and her unhappiness intensify. Given the presentation of Gertrude in Shakespeare's text, it is impossible to see the accuracy of Olivier's and Kozintsev's film presentations and of many stage depictions that show Gertrude shrinking after Act Three from Claudius's touch because of her newly awakened sense of de-cency and shame. Nor does the text suggest, as Olivier does in his film, that she is suspicious of the pearl that Claudius drops in Hamlet's wine goblet. Gertrude does not drink the wine to protect Hamlet or to kill herself because of her shame; she drinks it in her usual direct way to toast Hamlet's success in the fencing match, after first briskly and maternally advising him to wipe his face. In fact, Gertrude's death is symbolic of the internal disharmony caused by her divided loyalties. . . .

Gertrude's words and actions in Shakespeare's *Hamlet* create not the lusty, lustful, lascivious Gertrude that one generally sees in stage and film productions but a compliant, loving, unimaginative woman whose only concern is pleasing others. . . .

In creating Gertrude, Shakespeare clearly diverged from the sources he followed quite closely in other areas, making her of a piece with the rest of the play—that is, problematic. But Gertrude is problematic not because of layers of complexity or a dense texture such as that of Hamlet but because, as with the ghost, Shakespeare does not provide all the "answers," all the necessary clues that would allow one to put together her character and fully understand her speech, actions, and motivations. Still, Gertrude is not a flat, uninteresting character as a result of her limited range of responses and concerns. Gertrude's words and acts interest the audience because, obviously, she is of extreme interest to the combatants in the play—the ghost, Hamlet and Claudius—all of whom see her literally and in quite heightened terms as a sexual *object*. . . . This is still a stereotype, but a more positive one than that of the temptress and destroyer—self-indulgent and soulless. And certainly it more accurately reflects the Gertrude that Shakespeare created.

Laertes: An Impulsive but Earnest Young Aristocrat

Marvin Rosenberg

Laertes, Polonius's son and Ophelia's brother, is sometimes compared to Hamlet, partly because each wants revenge for his father's murder. There are also the natural similarities between the two young aristocrats growing up in a medieval royal court. As the distinguished scholar Marvin Rosenberg, a professor of dramatic arts at the University of California at Berkeley, points out here, both youths go away to school, Laertes to Paris and Hamlet to Wittenberg. And both young men have strong feelings for Ophelia. In his thoughtful analysis of Laertes's personality, Rosenberg shows that, despite such superficial similarities, Laertes and Hamlet are very different characters. And although Laertes has many noble qualities, he has, like the play's other major characters, his darker side, too.

Laertes is a dashing, romantic figure who excites striking, spectacular moments in the play. Not much attention has been paid to him by scholar-critics and theatre observers; for all his activity in the later acts, he is not much cursed with inward struggle—while being surrounded by others fascinating for their infernos of inwardness. After Laertes' brief, bright introduction in I,i and I,iii, he disappears from the play—and Denmark—until he returns at the head of a rebellion in IV,v. . . .

A Spoilt Youth

His beginning is almost all surface. The son of a powerful political figure in court [Polonius], he has servants, and the status and funds to return to France. He has seemed Frenchified

Reprinted from *The Masks of Hamlet*, by Marvin Rosenberg (Newark: University of Delaware Press, 1992), by permission of Associated University Presses, Cranbury, New Jersey.

in his dress, his gestures, in the rhythms of his speech. . . .

But the Frenchness Laertes has taken on must be characterization, not caricature. Shakespeare enjoys making fun of the French, but Laertes will have a serious part to play.

He now heads for Paris, perhaps as a student, though little mention is made of serious work there. Claudius gives him leave to go and enjoy himself; Polonius, preaching the long list of precepts, never mentions study. He does say to the spy he sends to watch the young man, "Let him ply his music"—which could mean "Let him have his fun," but possibly suggests one course of study, not too trying on the intellect. He has carried an instrument as he sets off. The contrast to Hamlet, from Laertes' first request to return to Paris, is unmistakable: the one at Wittenberg serious, studious, the one at Paris, not. Laertes, an old player's observation has it, "is not a brain part."

For Laertes to be conspicuously—though not obtrusively—different from Hamlet is one of the functions of the role: so one actor was praised for a "swift, impetuous Laertes who thoroughly understands the contrast he must offer to the vacillating Hamlet." But there is more to Laertes than difference; so, of another: "played usually as a brash and rather stupid young man, [he] was notably sensitive and intelligent." If Laertes' polyphony [contrasting facets of personality] is not as complex as the others, he does have dimension and subtext.

He tends, like the others, to lean toward sweetness or power, though again like the others, the most persuasive Laertes has elements of both.

The power Laertes is forceful in lecturing Ophelia in I,iii. He warns her rather than advises her; he instructs her rather than confides in her. His "My dear sister" is more admonishing than loving. Leading a rebellion over the killing of his father suits him, as does fighting at a grave, and duelling. But he must soften at the sight of Ophelia mad, must grieve, must weep, must feel some guilt at his conniving at a murder in the guise of a fair play. Some sense of the range in the role may be gathered from descriptives of various Laertes—most of them near the power extreme. Thus [noted British actor, John] Gielgud's: "vigorous," "swaggering," "upright and fiery," "a vivid force," "dashing," "electrifying," "a manly Laertes, only too willing to outshout the lively Hamlet," "a handsome, sullen Laertes," "explosive," "fiery and hysterical," "matching [Gielgud] in force.". . .

Laertes at this power end of the spectrum has drawn from critics and reviews such other descriptives as boisterous, bluff, wild, vehement, virile, strong, vindictive, cross-grained, insensitive, ambitious, temperamental, unbridled, crude, quick off the mark and quick in a quarrel; a spoilt youth like his father.

His Charisma and Popularity

Even the sweet Laertes, in high moments, must sound the power in the role. The polyphony encloses extremes: heart-felt brotherly love, violent retaliation against offence. . . . "But the loveliness is always fragile [remarks one scholar], threatened by interlaced figures of war and dread." *Fear,* . . . *Fear* . . . , Laertes preaches to his sister.

The mainly sweet Laertes, who will seem driven to his fe-rocity, attracts from reviewers softer descriptives: impulsive, tender, sincere, sympathetic, lyrical, noble, refined, fresh, brave, knightly, poignant, earnest, charming, naive, a tearful boy.

"Boy." Again age is most important. If Laertes is one of a group hardly come of age—a group set against the elders—his love and respect for his sister and his father, his hot-headed revolt, his compassion for the crazed Ophelia, and his readiness to fight the wronger of his family, will have a dif-ferent tone from the Laertes who acts from the more cynical point of some maturity. Where the latter speaks from some experience of the world, the "boy" is more often earnest, naive, and is more likely to be "sweet" even in his moments of power. Leading his rebellion, threatening royalty, con-spiring in a shameful trap for Hamlet, he may be more emo-tional than hard, more hurt than angry. And here, too, one subtextual grace note of the kind possible in all the other major characters, was noted by one reviewer: in the final duel, Laertes fought "more from suicidal impulse than a lust for revenge." Is anything of this involved in his ready sub-mission to Claudius' vile plotting? A symptom of weakness? Of dependence? Of a need to be guided? Of the unthinking man? Of a death wish?

As actor-readers, we build on stipulated qualities in the role. Laertes longs for the play-life in France. He is a brilliant fencer, perhaps too a musician. He has it in him to rouse and to lead an army of rebels, to break into the royal palace, apparently overpowering the King's Swiss mercenaries. Laertes' followers are supportive of him enough to want him King; unless they are shown to be a restless rabble, this is some comment on his charisma and popularity. Hamlet will call him a "very noble youth"—and this does not merely refer to rank. He evidently loves his father to be so outraged and ready to kill a King and dare damnation over the wrongful death. Damnation must mean something to this man who calls on the heavens, speaks of angel and devil, and would risk his own soul to kill his enemy in the church.

LAERTES WARNS OPHELIA ABOUT HAMLET

In this exchange from Act 1, Scene 3, Laertes warns his sister, Ophelia, not to become too involved with Hamlet, who will only end up hurting her.

    Enter Laertes and Ophelia, his sister.

LAERTES

My necessaries are embarked. Farewell.
And, sister, as the winds give benefit
And convey (is) assistant, do not sleep,
But let me hear from you.

OPHELIA   Do you doubt that?

LAERTES

For Hamlet, and the trifling of his favor,
Hold it a fashion and a toy in blood,
A violet in the youth of primy nature,
Forward, not permanent, sweet, not lasting,
The perfume and suppliance of a minute,
No more.

OPHELIA   No more but so?

LAERTES   Think it no more.

For nature, crescent, does not grow alone
In thews and (bulk,) but, as this temple waxes,
The inward service of the mind and soul
Grows wide withal. Perhaps he loves you now,
And now no soil nor cautel doth besmirch
The virtue of his will; but you must fear,
His greatness weighed, his will is not his own,
(For he himself is subject to his birth.)
He may not, as unvalued persons do,
Carve for himself, for on his choice depends
The safety and [the] health of this whole state.
And therefore must his choice be circumscribed
Unto the voice and yielding of that body

However Laertes admonishes Ophelia, he evidently loves her; his grief in her mad scene demands to be voiced tenderly—*O rose of May! / Dear maid—kind sister—sweet Ophelia.* With all Laertes' concern for his manly image, he cannot help but weep. . . .

HIS DARKER SIDE

Laertes, with his over-dedication to "honor," must inevitably feel guilty about the treacherous murder he undertakes—though that he has even considered it disgraces him, as he

---

Whereof he is the head. Then, if he says he loves
   you,
It fits your wisdom so far to believe it
As he in his particular act and place
May give his saying deed, which is no further
Than the main voice of Denmark goes withal.
Then weigh what loss your honor may sustain
If with too credent ear you list his songs
Or lose your heart or your chaste treasure open
To his unmastered importunity.
Fear it, Ophelia; fear it, my dear sister,
And keep you in the rear of your affection,
Out of the shot and danger of desire.
The chariest maid is prodigal enough
If she unmask her beauty to the moon.
Virtue itself 'scapes not calumnious strokes.
The canker galls the infants of the spring
Too oft before their buttons be disclosed,
And, in the morn and liquid dew of youth,
Contagious blastments are most imminent.
Be wary, then; best safety lies in fear.
Youth to itself rebels, though none else near.
OPHELIA
I shall the effect of this good lesson keep
As watchman to my heart. But, good my brother,
Do not, as some ungracious pastors do,
Show me the steep and thorny way to heaven,
Whiles, (like) a puffed and reckless libertine,
Himself the primrose path of dalliance treads
And recks not his own rede.
LAERTES   O, fear me not.

Barbara A. Mowat and Paul Werstine, eds., *Hamlet.* New York: Simon and Schuster, 1992, pp. 39–43.

knows. His first, instinctive reaction had been like Hamlet's: immediate revenge! But he too was brought to delay. How much because of Claudius' cunning subornation, how much from subtextual reluctance, will provide some measure of his depth. One sign of a cunning in him, of a readiness for stealth: he may ultimately stab suddenly from behind at an unguarded Hamlet. Most shameful of all, and an essential key to Laertes' darker side: he is ready to use *poison*. . . . A despised, "Italianate" weapon, it discolors Laertes as it stained Claudius. As actor-readers we need to ask ourselves: why . . . carry this dishonorable stuff? . . . Can we believe, does it soften the image, that at least the poison was obtained only after Laertes learned of Polonius' death? He does not say so. He has certainly become a different man since he first went back to France. Like all the other central characters, he undergoes transformation. So one theatre Laertes: "From a careless undergraduate to a young man of parts and passion." In another, a striking transformation "between the early cavalier and the sorrow-stricken and then penitent youth.". . . Laertes left a fresh boy; he returned from his voyage, as the Hamlet did from his, aged into a man. Like all caught between the mighty opposites, he is doomed to suffer.

Finally, a special problem for the actor. After the two early scenes when Laertes first appears and then leaves for Paris, he does not enter again for almost three full acts, when he bursts in at the head of a mob. Offstage he must save his energy and momentum for his outburst. Not easy. [Renowned American stage actor, Otis] Skinner, playing the role in a sustained run:

> The long stupefying wait in the bad air of the dressing room— over an hour and a half—robbed me of every particle of spirit. I employed violent calisthenics before the scene of fury.

That only worked for a while. Finally, he learned to go for a walk, just to get the fresh air.

CHAPTER 3

Themes and Ideas Developed in *Hamlet*

READINGS ON
HAMLET

Grief That Leads to Tragedy

Lily B. Campbell

In this excerpt from her book, *Shakespeare's Tragic Heroes*, the late and noted Shakespearean scholar, Lily B. Campbell, explains why she views Hamlet as a "study in the passion of grief." She begins with the observation that Hamlet, Laertes (Ophelia's brother), and Fortinbras (the prince of Norway, who is leading an army through Denmark on the way to attack Poland) are all young men grieving the deaths of their fathers. Campbell suggests that Hamlet's grief is so overpowering that his memory and will to act are impeded. This explains his delay in enacting revenge on his uncle. In Laertes' case, grief leads directly to rage and rash actions. Eventually, Campbell contends, these two grief-stricken characters meet head on and annihilate each other. Only in Fortinbras does the power of reason contain grief and allow the character to manage his affairs wisely. At the end of the play, he is the one who stands over the bodies of Hamlet and the others and takes charge of the Danish court.

The play of *Hamlet* is concerned with the story of three young men—Hamlet, Fortinbras, and Laertes—each called upon to mourn the death of a father, each feeling himself summoned to revenge wrongs suffered by his father. Grief in each for the loss of his father is succeeded by the desire for revenge. But each must act according to the dictates of his own temperament and his own humour.

The fundamental problem that Shakespeare undertook to answer in *Hamlet*, then, is the problem of the way men accept sorrow when it comes to them. And it is evident throughout the play that the grief of Fortinbras is being pre-

Reprinted from *Shakespeare's Tragic Heroes: Slaves of Passion*, by Lily B. Campbell (New York: Cambridge University Press, 1930), by permission of the publisher.

sented as a grief dominated by reason, while it is equally evident that the grief of Hamlet and Laertes is excessive grief
leading to destruction. That Hamlet himself saw in these two
other young men his own image, is of course, evident. Of the
resolute Fortinbras he exclaims in self-reproach:

> How all occasions do inform against me,
> And spur my dull revenge! . . .
>   Examples gross as earth exhort me;
> Witness this army of such mass and charge
> Led by a delicate and tender prince,
> Whose spirit with divine ambition puff'd
> Makes mouths at the invisible event,
> Exposing what is mortal and unsure
> To all that fortune, death, and danger dare,
> Even for an egg-shell. Rightly to be great
> Is not to stir without great argument,
> But greatly to find quarrel in a straw
> When honour's at the stake.

And of Laertes he says regretfully:

> For, by the image of my cause, I see
> The portraiture of his. . . .

In many respects and by nature Hamlet is like Fortinbras,
but he has been changed by grief into something different. . . .

GRIEF THAT MAKES REASON FAIL

If my analysis is correct, then, *Hamlet* becomes a study in
the passion of grief. In Hamlet himself it is passion which is
not moderated by reason, a passion which will not yield to
the consolations of philosophy. And being intemperate and
excessive grief, Hamlet's grief is, therefore, the grief that
makes memory fade, that makes reason fail in directing the
will, that makes him guilty of sloth. Yet Hamlet is capable of
an anger that demands revenge. His blood answered the
ghost's first demand with a swift promise; he could offend
Ophelia, kill Polonius, escape on shipboard, insult Laertes,
even kill the King in moments of unreasonable passion, but

> What to ourselves in passion we propose,
> The passion ending, doth the purpose lose,
> The violence of either grief or joy
> Their own enactures with themselves destroy.

Because in our own day we are sentimental about grief
and those that grieve, it is hard for us to get the Renaissance
point of view in regard to grief, a point of view which was in-

A REMARKABLE WARRIOR-PRINCE

Noted Shakespearean commentator Marvin Rosenberg of the University of California offers this analysis of Fortinbras's character, pointing out that, unlike Hamlet, he can act decisively and without hesitation.

This scene (with Fortinbras) was almost invariably cut, as far as we know, from Betterton through to Forbes-Robertson in the late nineteenth century; some twentieth century stagings also deleted it. A serious loss: we would miss this significant contrast between the man of war and the man of mind; between a trivial task done eagerly for glory and a solemn one undone; between a young general-prince directing an action abroad, and a prisoner-prince carried away to his death. And we would miss a pivotal soliloquy, a crucial turning point in Hamlet's character.

Consider the scene with the eyes of the naive spectator: the whole fate of the play is in the balance—will Hamlet now go to his death in England? What can he do?

At once we-audience see, in contrast to the endangered Hamlet, a Fortinbras committed without hesitation to action. Will he help Hamlet escape? Will Hamlet learn from him how to pursue his own objective, before it is too late? Is this Hamlet's last chance?

Fortinbras will be seen now only briefly, but in that time becomes for Hamlet a remarkable warrior-prince. Not an ideal philosopher, like Horatio, commingling blood and judgment, but a soldier who dares, who can be rash, eager—and competent—to pluck bright honor from the pale-faced moon. Who throws off shackles the elderly try to bind him with.

How well does Hamlet so judge Fortinbras that he will be ready to vote the Norweyan a king of Denmark? Such elevation seems hardly deserved by the Fortinbras of politically oriented stagings who becomes a monster of militarism—barely able to wait to take over Hamlet's kingdom—who rides roughshod over Denmark's remains in the last scene. But these portrayals thwart Shakespeare's lines. Hamlet, at his most reliable, sees a *delicate and tender prince*; and Fortinbras will indeed speak with some delicacy when he presides over the final catastrophe.

Marvin Rosenberg, *The Masks of Hamlet.* Newark: University of Delaware Press, 1992, p. 747.

herited from the Middle Ages as well as from the older classical philosophy. Shakespeare did not fail to see and to show the essential humanness of grief in its passionate refusal of the consolations of philosophy. Neither did he fail to show the destruction which followed Hamlet's slothfulness [slowness] in executing what his reason had judged and commanded him to do. Nor did he fail to show the destruction that came from his passionate and rash action when he acted from passion and not from reason.

Laertes, too, was the victim of excessive grief, but his grief was that which moved to rage. He, too, acted from passion and not from reason. Even in his killing of Hamlet he acted against the dictates of his own conscience, having promised to do so under the influence of violent passion, moved by grief to hate and by hate to revenge.

Ophelia is also the victim of excessive grief, her own and Hamlet's. And thus the toll of that passion which sins in failing to follow reason is complete.

THE KING'S AMBITION AND LUST

There is still to be reckoned the sin which is mortal, the sin which has come as the effect of passion which has perverted the will. Such is the acknowledged sin both of the King and the Queen. The King in his great soliloquy as he tries to pray sees himself accursed . . . and yet hopeful of mercy. But he cannot be forgiven while yet he holds the rewards of his deed, "My crown, mine own ambition, and my queen". The three objects of his passion, in themselves sinful, are thus indicative of the mortally sinful nature of the King's passion. These ends could not have been approved by reason unless reason was perverted. But more than that we see the King continuing to guide his passion and his action to the very last by a reason perverted to the choice of wrong ends. Ambition and lust have taken possession of the King until they have turned his reason into an instrument for their own uses, and until they have indeed turned his soul away from God into mortal sin. And though God's vengeance is slow, there is no doubt in the mind of any reader of *Hamlet* that the King has suffered punishment from the moment when he committed his crime,—in the fear and suspicion and unrest of his days, in the increasing battalions of his troubles, in the sick soul which could not rid itself of passion or of the fruits of passion to find peace with God. Nor can any reader doubt that the eternal vengeance of God is to fall upon the King.

FORTUNE'S PUPPETS

Shakespeare's picture of the Queen is explained to us by Hamlet's speech to her in her closet. There we see again the

picture of sin as evil willed by a reason perverted by passion,
for so much Hamlet explains in his accusation of his mother:

> You cannot call it love, for at your age
> The hey-day in the blood is tame, it's humble,
> And waits upon the judgement; and what judgement
> Would step from this to this? . . .
> O shame! where is thy blush? Rebellious hell,
> If thou canst mutine in a matron's bones,
> To flaming youth let virtue be as wax
> And melt in her own fire. Proclaim no shame
> When the compulsive ardour gives the charge,
> Since frost itself as actively doth burn
> And *reason panders will.*

And of the Queen's punishment as it goes on throughout the
play, there can be no doubt either. Her love for Hamlet, her
grief, the woes that come so fast that one treads upon the
heel of another, her consciousness of wrong-doing, her final
dismay are those also of one whose soul has become alien-
ated from God by sin.

It is here, it seems to me, that we see the true significance
of the play in its treatment of passion. Through passion
which has warped reason, so that "reason panders will", the
King and the Queen have come to the sin that is mortal.
Through passion undirected by reason, Hamlet, Laertes, and
Ophelia have brought havoc into the world, but theirs is not
mortal sin. Hamlet has failed to do what his reason has de-
creed that he should do; he has failed to kill the King. His
grief has made him sluggish, and he has allowed swift passion to seize him. The result is devastation but not eternal
damnation. And at the end of the play Fortinbras and Horatio live to dominate the scene, Fortinbras and Horatio being
the two characters in the play in whom reason has swayed
passion. Fortinbras has been called to grief for a father
whose honour he has undertaken to revenge, but his passion has yielded to reason, and his Poland expedition has
been undertaken for "divine ambition" and honour's sake.
Horatio is not passion's slave, but one in whom "blood and
judgement are so well commingled" that he is not a mere
pipe for Fortune to play upon. And this is but to say again
that those who balance passion by reason are not Fortune's
puppets. And such is the lesson of tragedy.

The Supernatural in *Hamlet*

Cumberland Clark

In his use of the ghost in *Hamlet*, Shakespeare effectively exploited the medieval beliefs about spirits and other manifestations of the supernatural that were still widely accepted in his day. For instance, ghosts were thought to appear shortly before the occurrence of a great crisis, usually to obtain revenge, exact justice, or warn the living about impending doom. Such specters were also said to entice humans to self-destruction. In this informative essay, the late Cumberland Clark, former vice president of the Shakespeare Reading Society and a prolific author on Shakespeare's works, discusses how Shakespeare carefully incorporated supernatural ideas and beliefs into *Hamlet*. He also briefly compares the use of the ghost in *Hamlet* to the use of the three witches in *Macbeth*, pointing out that the former tells about the past, while the latter reveal the future. However Shakespeare employed such supernatural elements, says Clark, he did so meaningfully and effectively.

At least six or seven years pass after the writing of *Midsummer Night's Dream* before we find Shakespeare engaged on *Hamlet*, the second of the great plays with an important Supernatural element, and, in the opinion of many, the greatest tragedy ever penned. What a profound change has come over his attitude towards the Unseen! No longer does he handle it in . . . [a] cheerful, jocular, irresponsible spirit. . . .

Shakespeare's attitude towards the Supernatural coincides, as we should expect, with his general view of life. He is in no mood now to deal with the empty, frivolous, meaningless little fairies. The form of the Supernatural, which he adopts at this stage, is the eerie, horrible, terrifying ghost. . . .

Reprinted from *Shakespeare and the Supernatural*, by Cumberland Clark (London: Williams and Norgate, 1931).

Once Shakespeare had decided to introduce a ghost into *Hamlet*—or rather, to retain the ghost he found in the old play upon which he worked—he set about endowing it with the dignity and convincingness which distinguished all his supernatural characters. As a dramatist he knew the need of clothing his spectre in all the current ghostly superstitions. His aim was not merely to entertain the less intelligent portion of his audience, important as he realized that to be; but, in the interests of his plot, to make the ghost appear real and possible to all. He meant to persuade even the most sceptical of the actual existence of ghosts, and presented his proofs with such assurance that most readers of the play cannot escape the feeling that the Poet was himself a firm believer in the visits of these eerie creatures to our Earth.

THE DANGERS OF CONFRONTING A GHOST

The *Hamlet* Ghost fulfils all the demands of popular superstition. In the first place it comes in strange and creepy circumstances, at dead of night, when it is cold and still and lonely.

> 'Tis now the very witching time of night,
> When churchyards yawn, and hell itself breathes out
> Contagion to this world.

> (III. 2. 405–407.)

It appears clad in the garments worn in mortal life. . . . Its appearance arouses the terror of the sentries on the platform before the castle at Elsinore. It cannot speak unless spoken to. This last was a very important point in Elizabethan ghost-lore. Not only were apparitions silent until addressed, but it needed an educated man to make them talk. All exorcists were supposed to be learned and fluent in the Latin tongue. Herein is the explanation of Marcellus's remark, "Thou art a scholar; speak to it, Horatio" (I. 1. 42). When persuaded to speak, the ghostly visitors confine themselves to their mission and its immediate purpose. Of life beyond the grave they are stubbornly reticent. When they do lift the curtain, it is a peep at hell they give us, not a peep at heaven. . . .

Ghosts were thought to appear before some great crisis in human affairs, to exact justice, to revenge a foul deed, to give a warning, to reveal hidden treasure, or otherwise perform the commands of the supernatural powers. After the first visit of the *Hamlet* spectre, Horatio and the soldiers try to determine its cause, and agree that the threat of war with Norway must be the explanation. This dialogue engages our attention and hints at the importance of the apparition. It enables us to believe in it, and assures us that the appearance is not frivolous and meaningless. When the Ghost meets Hamlet himself, we learn the true reason—"to revenge his foul and most unnatural murder" (I. 5. 25). . . .

Hamlet addresses the spirit, which beckons him to follow it. Horatio tries to dissuade the willing Prince, for ghosts were credited with the vile intention of enticing men to their self-destruction (I. 4. 69–74):

> What if it tempt you toward the flood, my lord,
> Or to the dreadful summit of the cliff
> That beetles o'er his base into the sea
> And there assume some other horrible form,
> Which might deprive your sovereignty of reason
> And draw you into madness? . . .

Hamlet obeys the Ghost's command to follow him, ignoring the protest of Horatio, who is much relieved, on coming up with him later, to find him safe.

A GHOST THAT IS TRUE TO TYPE

Despite his long conversation with the Ghost and the justification of his own feelings of depression, Hamlet cannot shake off his old beliefs and feel convinced that the apparition was in very truth his father returned from the dead. The call to revenge falls on doubting ears and results in hesitancy and inaction. In his long soliloquy at the end of Act II, the Prince says (II. 2. 627–632):

> The spirit that I have seen
> May be the devil; and the devil hath power
> To assume a pleasing shape; yea, and perhaps
> Out of my weakness and my melancholy,
> As he is very potent with such spirits,
> Abuses me to damn me.

Therefore he decides to stage the interlude in order to make the king himself betray his guilt. Only when this trick succeeds, does he say to Horatio, "I'll take the ghost's word" (III. 2. 298) and really believes at last that his father has communicated with him. On the later appearance of the Ghost in Gertrude's closet he admits the relationship and asks, "Do you not come your tardy son to chide?" (III. 4. 106).

In *Hamlet,* then, Shakespeare gives us a ghost that is true to type, a ghost that makes every important concession to prevalent superstition, even adopting the more popular notion as to its origin, after toying with and rejecting the more scholarly construction of an emanation from the Evil One.

Nothing could be more masterly than Shakespeare's treatment of the *Hamlet* Ghost. Such is his skill that he makes the impossible appear real and convincing. . . . Modern audiences, comparatively free of the shackles of Elizabethan superstition, are still thrilled by the Ghost and do not regard it as ridiculous. This is an achievement beyond the power of any dramatist who is not a genius.

The popularity of the Supernatural on the Shakespearean stage was so great that . . . some playwrights were tempted to introduce ghosts and witches even when quite extraneous to [had nothing to do with] their plots. Shakespeare was never guilty of this artistic blunder, although there is evidence that he was pressed at times to introduce pieces of pageantry, which could quite easily, and perhaps with advantage, have been omitted. Contemporary dramatists treated the Supernatural with much less dignity and respect than Shakespeare. They were far less restrained. They brought their immortals on to the stage at random and allowed them to mix casually with their human characters. Shakespeare knew the error of this—knew that by so doing the illusion was entirely destroyed. . . .

Characteristic of Shakespeare's treatment is the aloofness of *Hamlet* Ghost. It appears to ignore the existence of the soldiers. Even when the scholarly Horatio addresses it, it declines to answer until it delays too long and the cock crows. When it refuses to obey the order to halt and the sentries strike at it with their halberds, it eludes them easily and vanishes. On its next appearance, it refuses to speak to Hamlet while he is with his companions. Only when it has beckoned him to a place apart does it deliver its vital message. In the later appearance, in Gertrude's chamber, it is more distant still, and the fleshly minded queen cannot see it at all.

THE SUPERNATURAL'S POWERS LIMITED

The importance of the Ghost in the unfolding of the plot of *Hamlet* will be apparent to all students of drama. Its revelations summarize briefly the previous history of Denmark and put the audience in possession of facts which it is essential they should know. As the play proceeds, we find the Ghost's story gradually confirmed and see the evil results of adultery and murder. Here we may note a contrast with the tragedy of *Macbeth.* In *Hamlet* the Supernatural reveals the *past* and is corroborated: in *Macbeth* it reveals the *future,* and its prophecies are fulfilled. There is a further difference of first importance. In the Scottish tragedy the Weird Sisters succeed in persuading Macbeth to carry out their designs: in *Hamlet* the Ghost really fails in his mission, for the Prince hesitates, doubts, and delays, and finally is moved to kill the murderer by other causes altogether. The Weird Sisters do not return to Macbeth to lead him further into the mire. They are apparently satisfied with the mischief they have already done. It is only when Macbeth comes of his own free will to consult them that they continue their game of treacherous, misleading prophecy. The Ghost in *Hamlet,* however, is forced to return to whet his son's "almost blunted purpose" (III. 4. 111).

An important question arises here as to the extent of the power of the Supernatural over mortal men and women. A study of the two plays *Hamlet* and *Macbeth* suggests that its influence is only limited. Man is ever his own master, always able to exercise his sovereign free-will. Ghosts and witches can only suggest, tempt, persuade, and appeal; they cannot command, nor compel. . . .

How circumscribed [limited] was the power of ghosts is clearly shown in *Hamlet.* They return to Earth with a special duty to perform, but they cannot accomplish this duty by their own efforts alone. They are compelled to work through a human personality. The Ghost had no power to float into the Castle at Elsinore and slay Claudius with its own hands. It must choose the living Hamlet as an instrument; and even then, it could not insist on his carrying out the task of revenge. It could only spur him on in the hope that the deed would be done. . . .

OBJECTIVE VERSUS SUBJECTIVE USE OF GHOSTS

Shakespeare uses two kinds of ghosts in his dramas, the objective and the subjective. The objective ghost is intended to be really present and is seen by several people at once. Hamlet's Ghost is objective, for it manifests itself to all those who happen to be on the platform at the moment. Bernardo and Marcellus, and the men under them, are matter-of-fact soldiers, not at all the type liable to psychical experiences. They are upset when the sceptical Horatio makes light of their story and taxes them with imagining things. Marcellus observes (I. 1. 23–25):

> Horatio says 'tis but our fantasy;
> And will not let belief take hold of him,
> Touching this dreaded sight, twice seen of us.

Therefore they bring him along to the platform so that he may see for himself and change his opinion of them. The Ghost obligingly reappears, and the unbeliever is convinced by the testimony of his own senses (56–58):

> I might not this believe
> Without the sensible and true avouch
> Of mine own eyes.

By these means the reality of the *Hamlet* Ghost is attested. Shakespeare means us to accept it as an actual manifestation. It is an objective ghost, not a trick of the imagination caused by terror, worry, or madness, nor the unsubstantial product of a dream. These last were the common conditions in which subjective ghosts were seen, such a ghost being visible only to the person whom it closely concerned. It was when Macbeth was in the grip of guilty fear that he saw the Ghost of Banquo. It was during his troubled sleep on the eve of Bosworth that Richard III was visited by the spirits of his slain. It was when Brutus was obsessed with a premonition of his own death that he saw the shade of Caesar. Shakespeare, indeed, made more use of the subjective than the objective ghost. It would seem that the *Hamlet* Ghost itself becomes subjective on its appearance in Gertrude's closet, for while Hamlet talks with it, the Queen can see nothing. She accepts the common explanation of Hamlet's behaviour and believes (III. 4. 137–139):

> This is the very coinage of your brain:
> This bodiless creation ecstasy
> Is very cunning in. . . .

MESSENGERS FROM THE UNSEEN

In Belleforest's French translation of the story of Hamlet from the Latin of the Danish historian, Saxo Grammaticus, no mention of a ghost occurs. There is no doubt, however, that there was an older tragedy of *Hamlet*, probably written by Kyd, upon which the Shakespearean play was based, and this earlier piece apparently contained a ghost. . . .

There seems little doubt that Shakespeare took the appearance of the Ghost in Act I of *Hamlet* from Kyd's play. The long speeches in Scene V with their invective and moralization are not at all characteristic of the Shakespearean ghosts, who are usually the most reticent of beings. Shakespeare in this part of the play was probably rewriting Kyd. The second appearance of the *Hamlet* Ghost presents an extraordinary contrast with the first. On this occasion (III. 4) the Ghost limits itself to half a dozen lines, four of which refer to the Queen and have little to do with the purpose of its reappearance. This is more typical of Shakespeare's use of this particular form of the Supernatural. We draw the conclusion, then, that while Kyd furnished the groundwork for the first visit of the spectre, the second visit was Shakespeare's own invention. . . .

Ghosts were [valuable] to Shakespeare in his work of providing plays for the multitude. . . . We cannot fail to be impressed by his sparing use of the Supernatural and his refusal to be tempted to introduce so sensational a feature without real dramatic purpose. He was always careful to give his ghosts an essential part to play and never introduced them as meaningless supernumeraries [walk-ons or extras]. The *Hamlet* Ghost, like the Weird Sisters of *Macbeth* and the spirit of *Julius Caesar*, dominates the whole action, and controls the fortunes and characters of all who come beneath its influence. Hamlet is a changed man after his eerie experience; and his own violent death, as well as the tragedies of Polonius, Ophelia, Gertrude, Laertes, and Claudius, is to be directly attributed to the spectre's intervention. [Scholar] Mary A. Woods, writing on Shakespeare's ghosts generally, says, "They are no mere stage accessories. They have a function and a dignity that compel the awestruck recognition of the most careless. They are Messengers from the Unseen, Ministers of Justice, Avengers of crimes that but for them might have remained unpunished.". . .

The Ghost in *Hamlet* is an instructive case of the effective employment of the spectral in dramatic craftmanship, and an excellent example of the skill with which Shakespeare endowed his supernatural beings with all the prevalent superstitions. But it is more than that. It is a revelation of the inner Shakespeare and his changing and darkening mental attitude towards the Unseen at the beginning of his middle life and his great tragic period.

A Court and World Infected by the Disease of Corruption

Rebecca West

In this essay, one of the most famous written about *Hamlet*, noted Shakespearean critic Rebecca West suggests that Hamlet's world is corrupt and that he is "disgusted by his own kind." West draws an unsavory, although not totally unsympathetic, portrait of Ophelia, contending that the young woman is a potent symbol of the corruption that plagues the Danish royal court. In this view, Ophelia is used, much like an object, by her father (Polonius) and others for political and other purposes; while Ophelia herself is unable to resist becoming tainted by the evil of her abusers. Of all the main characters, says West, only Hamlet is able to rise above the immoral mire of his kind, although even he does so only in his last moments on the polluted earth.

Hamlet recognizes the value of tradition. That is made clear by the courage he shows in choosing to meet the ghost and in casting off the hands of his companions when it bids him follow it and they seek to hold him back. But he feels no real reverence for tradition. That is a very strange scene, when he swears his companions to secrecy on his sword, and the ghost raps upward on the earth they stand on, and Hamlet says, "You hear this fellow in the cellarage" (I.5.151). The root of this disrespect becomes explicable when we inquire into Hamlet's attitude to humanity. For tradition is the distillation of human experience, and it must be condemned if humanity is condemned; and Hamlet was disgusted by his own kind.

THE SLIME OF SEXUAL CORRUPTION

There are other crimes afoot in Elsinore, in the world, as well as murder. The ghost wishes Hamlet to avenge his mur-

Reprinted from *The Court and the Castle*, by Rebecca West (New Haven, CT: Yale University Press, 1957), by permission of the publisher. Copyright 1957 by Yale University Press, Inc.

der and also to put an end to the unholy offense of the marriage between his widow and his murderer. But when Hamlet talks of these matters with his mother he loses all interest in that part of the command which relates to his father's murder, and in the course of over eighty lines addressed to her he devotes only three to a perfunctory mention of the fact that her present husband murdered her previous husband, and when she shows that she did not know that any such crime had been committed he does not take the opportunity of enlightening her. He simply tells her that she is behaving reprehensibly in living with her present husband, not because he had murdered her dead husband and his own brother, but because he was not so good looking as her dead husband. It is not surprising, though it is always comic, that the ghost should then reappear in order to ask Hamlet to stick to the point. "Do not forget: this visitation is but to whet thy almost blunted purpose" (III.4.110). But a revelation is made in the course of the scene. The Queen admits the charge of sensuality (III.4.88):

> Oh, Hamlet, speak no more,
> Thou turn'st mine eyes into my very soul,
> And there I see such black and grained spots
> As will not leave their tinct.

Claudius is guilty, the Queen is guilty, and so as this scene makes quite plain, is Hamlet. All that he says is smeared with a slime which is the mark of sexual corruption. . . .

OPHELIA DISREPUTABLE?

That has been indicated earlier in the play by his scenes with Ophelia. There is no more bizarre aspect of the misreading of Hamlet's character than the assumption that his relations with Ophelia were innocent and that Ophelia was a correct and timid virgin of exquisite sensibilities. . . . She was not a chaste young woman. That is shown by her tolerance of Hamlet's obscene conversations, which cannot be explained as consistent with the custom of the time. If that were the reason for it, all the men and women in Shakespeare's plays, Romeo and Juliet, Beatrice and Benedict, Miranda and Ferdinand, Antony and Cleopatra, would have talked obscenely together, which is not the case. "The marriage of true minds" would hardly, even in the most candid age, have expressed itself by this ugly chatter. . . . The truth is that Ophelia was a disreputable young woman: not scandalously so, but still disreputable. She was foredoomed to it by her father. . . . Polonius is interesting because he was a cunning old intriguer who, like an iceberg, only showed one-eighth of himself above the surface. The innocuous [harmless] sort of worldly wisdom that rolled off his tongue in butter balls was a very small part of what he knew. It has been insufficiently noted that Shakespeare would never have held up the action in order that Polonius should give his son advice as to how to conduct himself abroad, unless the scene helped him to develop his theme. But "This above all—to thine own self be true; And it must follow, as the night the day, Thou canst not then be false to any man" (I.3.78), has considerable . . . value when it is spoken by an old gentleman who is presently going to instruct a servant to spy on his son, and to profess great anxiety about his daughter's morals, when plainly he needed to send her away into the country if he really wanted her to retain any. . . .

The girl is not to be kept out of harm's way. She is a card that can be played to take several sorts of tricks. . . . Surely Ophelia is one of the few authentic portraits of that army of not virgin martyrs, the poor little girls who were sacrificed to family ambition in the days when a court was a cat's cradle of conspiracies. Man's persuasion that his honor depends on the chastity of his womenfolk has always been liable to waste away and perish within sight of a throne. Particularly where monarchy had grown from a yeasty mass of feudalism, few families found themselves able to resist the temptation to hawk any young beauty in their brood, if it seemed likely that she might catch the eye of the king or any man close to the king. Unfortunately the king's true favorite was usually not a woman but an ideology. If royal approval was withdrawn from the religious or political faith held by the family which had hawked the girl, she was as apt to suffer fatality as any of her kinsmen. The axe has never known chivalry. . . .

Ophelia has lost her integrity. She fiddles with the truth when she speaks of Hamlet to her father, and she fiddles with the truth when she talks to Hamlet as her father and Claudius eavesdrop; and she contemplates without surprise or distaste Hamlet's obscenity, the scab on his spiritual sore.

THE WHOLE COURT DESTROYED HER

Surely the picture of Ophelia shows that Shakespeare, who wrote more often of cruelty than any other great writer, was not a cruel man, and was great in pity, that rare emotion. He shows the poor little creature, whom the court had robbed of her honesty, receiving no compensation for the loss, but being driven to madness and done to death. For the myth which has been built round Hamlet is never more perverse than when it pretends that Ophelia went mad for love and killed herself. No line in the play suggests that she felt either passion or affection for Hamlet. She never mentions him in the mad scene, and Horatio says of her, "She speaks much of her father." Indeed she was in a situation which requires no sexual gloss. Her father had been murdered by a member of the royal house, and she found herself without protection, since her brother Laertes was in France, in the midst of a crisis such as might well send her out of her wits with fear. For the Danes hostile to the royal house made of her wrong a new pretext for their hostility, and the royal house, noting this, turned against her, helpless though she was. . . .

Courts thus threatened had their own ways of dealing with the threats, as all courtiers knew; and Shakespeare must have heard of women thus dealt with who had been frightened into madness. . . .

It was the whole court that had destroyed her. She was a victim of society, which abandons principle for statecraft, for politics, for intrigue, because of its too urgent sense that it must survive at all costs, and in its panic loses cognizance of all the essentials by which it lives. Even her brother Laertes was not fully aware of his sister's tragedy, for he was tainted with the vice which Shakespeare feared most as a distraction: he was subject to lust. . . .

THE RACE'S ROOTS ARE EVIL?

It is Shakespeare's contention that the whole of the court is corrupt: society is corrupt. There is a flaw running horizontally through humanity wherever it is gathered together in space. It would seem natural therefore that Hamlet should obey the ghost and punish Claudius, who controls the court, who is an emblem of society. But the flaw runs vertically also; it runs through time, into the past. For Hamlet's father, the ghost, is in purgatory, doing penance for his sins, which were of the same gross kind as those he desires his son to punish. Shakespeare tells us this, stating the fact, and again using bombast to suggest immoderation (I.5.9):

> I am thy father's spirit,
> Doom'd for a certain term to walk the night,
> And for the day confined to fast in fires,
> Till the foul crimes done in my days of nature
> Are burnt and purged away. . . .

The ghost was indeed a sinner; the voice of tradition speaks from a tainted source. The evil in the world is not the product of the specially corrupt present generation, it has its roots in the generations that went before and also were corrupt; it has its roots in the race. There is no use pretending that we can frustrate our sinful dispositions by calling on tradition, because that also is the work of sinful man. This is the situation of our kind as it is shown to us in *Hamlet,* which is as pessimistic as any great work of literature ever written. . . .

THE BEAUTY OF THE WORLD

What does Shakespeare see written on the other side of the ledger? Nothing but beauty. This is the play which more than any of the others reminds us of the extraordinary advantages which he enjoyed. For it was his luck to see the human race at one of the moments, in one of the places, when it blossomed into a state of exceptional glory; and he moved among men and women who were beautiful, intelligent, learned, and fearless beyond the habit of our kind, and whose way of life, with its palaces and its pageants, was a proper setting for the jewels that they were. . . . It happened that the Renaissance man was observed by Shakespeare. "What a piece of work is man! How noble in reason! How infinite in faculty! In form and moving how express and admirable! In action how like an angel! In apprehension how like a god! The beauty of the world! The paragon of animals!" (II.2.305). Here is a coincidence. Shakespeare was himself "the paragon of animals," therefore he could describe to us the man who was "the beauty of the world." He could write this description and make the whole character of Hamlet as shown from scene to scene bear out what he said about man.

All through the play Hamlet speaks with a quick, springing harmony recognizable as the voice of physical and mental splendor; his mind travels like lightning yet strikes below the surface, and is impulsive not in surrender to folly but in search of wisdom. . . . In fact, Shakespeare has given us a picture of the Renaissance man . . . a being so gifted that he needs no supernatural being to raise him above the common lot. But Shakespeare, the supreme artist observing this supreme man, immediately adds, "And yet to me what is the quintessence of dust?" And his genius has been asking that question throughout the play. Scene after scene has demonstrated the paragon of animals to be an animal, the world to be so diseased that even its beauty is infected. This speech of homage to man is indeed an example of teasing ambiguity; it can be read without irony or with irony; each reading is equally faithful to the text.

Shakespeare hopes for little from the dust. It is quite certain that he wished to present Hamlet as a bad man, because he twice makes him rejoice at the thought of murdering men who had not made their peace with God. . . .

But to this bad man Shakespeare ascribes one virtuous action; and the nature of that action is determined by his most lasting preoccupation. It is a political action. Hamlet gives his dying breath to thought for the future of his people; his last words choose a ruler for them (V.2.343):

> O, I die, Horatio
> The potent poison quite o'ercrows my spirit;
> I cannot live to hear the news from England;
> But I do prophesy th' election lights
> On Fortinbras: he has my dying voice. . . .

Hamlet was never more the Renaissance man—who was a statesman . . . a prince careful for the safety of his subjects. Even if one be disillusioned with the race, and suspect paragons and the beauty of the world, this is still admirable. These fragile creatures, so little changed from dust that they constantly revert to it, show bravery in their intention that their species shall survive as if it were marble. Yet, all the same, how horrid is the sphere in which they show their excellence. The court was saved by its political conscience; yet it was damned by it too.

None Can Escape Death, the "Undiscovered Country"

Michael Neill

One of the most important underlying themes of *Hamlet*
is death, which the characters find themselves dealing
with repeatedly, both literally and symbolically. Shakespeare begins and ends the play with images of death:
the ghost in the opening scenes and the body-littered
throne room in the finale. And the rest of the piece frequently emphasizes the idea that all the characters, and
indeed all human beings, are trapped in a never-ending
cycle of birth and death.

Perhaps the most obvious and famous scene depicting this
theme is Act 5, Scene 1, the so-called "Gravedigger scene," sin-
gled out in this brief but pointed essay by Shakespearean
scholar Michael Neill. In confronting the rows of skulls un-
earthed by the diggers, Hamlet must confront his own ultimate
end and thus his own mortality. He too, he realizes, will one
day end up like Yorick, the court jester whose skull he holds in
his hand. Even the mightiest mortals, like the legendary
Alexander the Great, inevitably succumb to death in the end
and thus become part of the cycle of "dust-to-dust." As Neill
hints here, in watching this scene Shakespeare's audiences
would have been reminded of the ghastly imagery of the *Danse
Macabre*, or Dance of Death. This was a medieval European
folk story, depicted often in morality plays and paintings, in
which the dead rise and, in a frenzied dance, lead new victims
to the "undiscovered country from which no traveler returns."

How we respond to the ending of *Hamlet*—both as revenge
drama and as psychological study—depends in part on how we
respond to [the most important underlying theme] of the play—
that is, to *Hamlet* as a prolonged meditation on death. The play

From Michael Neill's essay "*Hamlet*: A Modern Perspective," reprinted, with minor
editing, with the permission of Washington Square Press Publication of Pocket Books,
a division of Simon & Schuster, from *The Tragedy of Hamlet, Prince of Denmark* (The
New Folger Library Shakespeare), by William Shakespeare, edited by Barbara A.
Mowat and Paul Werstine. Copyright © 1992 by The Folger Shakespeare Library.

is virtually framed by two encounters with the dead: at one end is the Ghost, at the other a pile of freshly excavated skulls. The skulls (all but one) are nameless and silent; the Ghost has an identity (though a "questionable" one) and a voice; yet they are more alike than might at first seem. For this ghost, though invulnerable "as the air," is described as a "dead corse," a "ghost . . . come from the grave," its appearance suggesting a grotesque disinterment [digging up] of the buried king (1.4.52–57; 1.5.139). The skulls for their part may be silent, but Hamlet plays upon each to draw out its own "excellent voice" ("That skull had a tongue in it and could sing once": 5. 1.77–78), just as he engineered that "miraculous organ" of the Ghost's utterance, the "Mousetrap."

There is a difference, however: Hamlet's dressing up the skulls with shreds of narrative ("as if 'twere Cain's jawbone . . . This might be the pate of a politician . . . or of a courtier . . . Why may not that be the skull of a lawyer": 5.1.78–101) only serves to emphasize their mocking anonymity [unknown identities], until the Gravedigger offers to endow one with a precise historical identity: "This same skull . . . was . . . Yorick's skull, the King's jester" (5.1.186–87). Hamlet is delighted: now memory can begin its work of loving resurrection. But how does the Gravedigger *know*? The answer is that of course he cannot; and try as Hamlet may to cover this bare bone with the flesh of nostalgic recollection, he cannot escape the wickedly punning reminder of "this *same* skull" that all skulls indeed look frightfully the same. Ironically, even Yorick's distinctive trademark, his grin, has become indistinguishable from the mocking leer of that grand jester of the *Danse Macabre*, Death the Antic: "Where be your gibes now? . . . Not one now to mock your own grinning?"; so that even as he holds it, the skull's identity appears to drain away. . . . It might as well be Alexander the Great's; or Caesar's; or anyone's. It might as well be what it will one day become—a handful of clay, fit to stop a beer barrel.

A GRAVE PREPARED FROM BIRTH

It is significant that (with the trivial exception of 4.4) the graveyard scene is the only one to take place outside the confines of Claudius's castle-prison. As the "common" place to which all stories lead, the graveyard both *invites* narrative and *silences* it. Each blank skull at once poses and confounds the question with which the tragedy itself began, "Who's there?," subsuming all human differences in awful likeness: "As you are now," goes the tombstone verse, "so once was I / As I am now, so shall you be." In the graveyard all stories collapse into one reductive history ("Alexander died, Alexander was buried, Alexander returneth to dust": 5.1.216–17). In this sense the Gravedigger is the mocking counterpart of the Player: and the houses of oblivion that gravediggers make challenge the players' memorial art by lasting "till doomsday" (5.1.61). Hamlet shares with the Gravedigger the same easy good-fellowship he extends to the play's other great outsider, the First Player; but the Gravedigger asserts a more sinister kind of intimacy with his claim to have begun his work "that very day that young Hamlet was born" (5.1.152–53). In this moment he identifies himself as the Prince's mortal double, the Sexton Death from the *Danse Macabre* who has been preparing him a grave from the moment of birth.

HAMLET CONFRONTS YORICK AND ALEXANDER

This is the core section of the famous Gravedigger scene from the play. Hamlet's simple question about how long it takes a buried body to rot leads to the discovery of the skull of a court jester he once knew and finally to the ironic realization that even the great Alexander could not escape the same fate.

Ham.　How long will a man lie i' th' earth ere he rot?

1. Clo.　Faith, if 'a be not rotten before 'a die—as we have many pocky corses, that will scarce hold the laying in—'a will last you some eight year or nine year. A tanner will last you nine year.

Ham.　Why he more than another?

1. Clo.　Why, sir, his hide is so tann'd with his trade that 'a will keep out water a great while, and your water is a sore decayer of your whoreson dead body. Here's a skull now hath lien you i' th' earth three and twenty years.

Ham.　Whose was it?

1. Clo.　A whoreson mad fellow's it was. Whose do you think it was?

Ham.　Nay, I know not.

1. Clo.　A pestilence on him for a mad rogue! 'a pour'd a flagon of Rhenish on my head once. This same skull, sir, was, sir, Yorick's skull, the King's jester.

Ham.　This?　　　　　　　　　　　　[*Takes the skull.*]

1. Clo.　E'en that.

Ham.　Alas, poor Yorick! I knew him, Horatio, a fellow of

ALWAYS THE WRONG STORY

If there is a final secret to be revealed, then, about that "undiscovered country" on which Hamlet's imagination broods, it is perhaps only the Gravedigger's spade that can uncover it. For his digging lays bare the one thing we can say for certain lies hidden "within" the mortal show of the flesh—the emblems of Death himself . . . who shadows each of us. . . . If there is a better story, one that would confer on the rough matter of life the consolations of form and significance, it is, the play tells us, one that cannot finally be told; for it exists on the other side of language, to be tantalizingly glimpsed only at the point when Hamlet is about to enter the domain of the inexpressible. The great and frustrating achievement of this play, its most ingenious and tormenting trick, the source of its endlessly belabored mystery, is to persuade us that such a story

---

infinite jest, of most excellent fancy. He hath bore me on his back a thousand times, and now how abhorr'd in my imagination it is! my gorge rises at it. Here hung those lips that I have kiss'd I know not how oft. Where be your gibes now, your gambols, your songs, your flashes of merriment, that were wont to set the table on a roar? Not one now to mock your own grinning—quite chop-fall'n. Now get you to my lady's [chamber], and tell her, let her paint an inch thick, to this favor she must come; make her laugh at that. Prithee, Horatio, tell me one thing.

    Hor. What's that, my lord?

    Ham. Dost thou think Alexander look'd a' this fashion i' th' earth?

    Hor. E'en so.

    Ham. And smelt so? pah! [*Puts down the skull.*]

    Hor. E'en so, my lord.

    Ham. To what base uses we may return, Horatio! Why may not imagination trace the noble dust of Alexander, till 'a find it stopping a bunghole?

    Hor. 'Twere to consider too curiously, to consider so.

    Ham. No, faith, not a jot, but to follow him tither with modesty enough and likelihood to lead it: Alexander died, Alexander was buried, Alexander returneth to dust, the dust is earth, of earth we make loam, and why of that loam whereto he was converted might they not stop a beer-barrel?

    The Riverside Shakespeare. Boston: Houghton and Mifflin, 1974, p. 1179.

might exist, while demonstrating its irreducible hiddenness. The only story Hamlet is given is that of a hoary old revenge tragedy, which he persuades himself (and us) can never denote him truly; but it is a narrative frame that nothing (not even inaction) will allow him to escape. The story of our lives, the play wryly acknowledges, is always the wrong story; but the rest, after all, is silence.

Hamlet's Christian Beliefs Stifle His Heroic Impulse

Paul A. Cantor

In this perceptive essay, University of Virginia
scholar Paul A. Cantor explores the theme of Christianity that permeates *Hamlet* and profoundly affects
the thoughts and actions of the main character. Cantor carefully explains the difference between classical (ancient Greek or Roman) heroes, who were pa-
gans, and more modern, Christian characters like
Hamlet. The attitudes and world views of classical
heroes like Achilles, the hero of Homer's *Iliad* (the
saga of the legendary Trojan War) and Brutus, one of
the Roman senators who assassinated Julius Caesar,
Cantor points out, were very different from Hamlet's.
Achilles and Brutus were preoccupied with earthly
life and did not allow concerns about an afterlife to
sway their actions. Hamlet, by contrast, is con-
strained by his Christian beliefs about a mysterious
afterlife and possible divine retribution for certain
earthly actions. Thus, he fatally hesitates and in the
end, unlike Achilles and Brutus, he is not all that
sure about what he was fighting for and why.

One might formulate what distinguishes Hamlet from a classical hero in many ways, but one can begin from this basic
point: his cosmos is not that of Achilles. The Greek hero
lives in a universe with finite horizons: he knows that he is
mortal and that death offers at most an existence as a bloodless shade [spirit], an existence to which life on earth even
as a slave is preferable (as Achilles's shade reveals in the
Odyssey). His singleminded determination as a warrior is related to his sense of his mortality. Because he knows that his
fate is to die young, he realises that he has only a brief period

Reprinted from *Shakespeare: "Hamlet"* by Paul Cantor, © 1989 Cambridge University
Press, by permission of Cambridge University Press.

of time to win glory for himself. Indeed, the only meaningful form of immortality his world offers him is the survival of his name through fame.

HAMLET'S MYSTERIOUS COSMOS

Hamlet, by contrast, living in the modern Christian world, believes that his soul is immortal (I.iv.65–8). This may seem like an obvious point, but it has wide-ranging implications for our understanding of Shakespeare's play. In fact, it is remarkable how many of the complications of Hamlet's situation can be traced to the impact his belief in an afterlife has on his thinking. From the very beginning he is preoccupied with the afterlife because from the very beginning he is preoccupied with suicide. Suicide is the issue on which Shakespeare demonstrates most clearly his awareness of the distinction between ancient, pagan heroes and modern, Christian ones. From our perspective, suicide is a surprisingly unproblematic notion for Shakespeare's Romans. Their ethic demands suicide from them when dishonour and disgrace are the alternative. Because they view it as a noble deed, they do not hesitate to commit suicide when the time comes. This is true even in the case of Brutus, a character often compared to Hamlet as a thoughtful, meditative man, who has difficulty making up his mind. But Brutus approaches his suicide with a firm resolve. Whatever his temperamental affinities with Hamlet may be, he has a diametrically opposed attitude towards suicide. This difference is not to be explained in terms of what we would today call contrasting 'personalities', but rather in terms of the contrasting regimes under which Brutus and Hamlet live. Brutus's regime virtually mandates suicide for a noble man under certain circumstances, whereas Hamlet's forbids it under any circumstances.

The first words we hear Hamlet speaking alone reveal him running up against the Christian prohibition of suicide:

> O that this too too solid flesh would melt,
> Thaw, and resolve itself into a dew!
> Or that the Everlasting had not fix'd
> His canon 'gainst self-slaughter.

> (I.ii.129–32)

These opening lines supply the keynote of Hamlet's character: throughout the play he shows a distinctive concern with the everlasting as opposed to the merely temporal. This orientation means that he cannot view action from the perspective of a classical hero. Unlike Achilles, he must consider whether his actions will lead him to be saved or damned. The fact that an eternity is at stake in his deeds gives him good reason to pause and consider their consequences. But the complications introduced into Hamlet's thinking by his belief in an afterlife run deeper than this. His Christianity opens a window on eternity, but it is a dark window. The most striking fact about the afterlife for Hamlet is that he cannot know with certainty what it will be like. His cosmos is far more mysterious than Achilles's. His belief in the immortality of the soul vastly raises the stakes involved in heroic action but, given the uncertainties surrounding life after death, it simultaneously makes it more difficult to calculate the consequences of such action.

VENGEANCE IS MINE

This is the main burden of Hamlet's most famous speech, the 'To be, or not to be' soliloquy. He reveals that he would have no difficulty in embracing suicide if he were a pagan, that is, if he believed that death is effectively the end of life. But he is troubled by visions of what lies beyond the finite horizons to which the ancient world was limited:

> For in that sleep of death what dreams may come
> When we have shuffled off this mortal coil,
> Must give us pause.

(III.i.65–7)

'The dread of something after death' grips Hamlet all the more powerfully because he realises that we must take on faith any claims about 'the undiscovr'd country, from whose bourn / No traveller returns' (III.i.77–9). He dwells on how belief in an afterlife alters the terms of heroic action and threatens to redirect and even stifle heroic impulses:

> thus the native hue of resolution
> Is sicklied o'er with the pale cast of thought,
> And enterprises of great pitch and moment
> With this regard their currents turn awry,
> And lose the name of action. . . .

(III.i.83–7)

Hamlet's other-worldly perspective would complicate his view of any heroic action, but it makes the task of revenge particularly complex. Paradoxically, even while forbidding revenge, Christianity offers a pattern of revenge more sinister than anything imagined in classical antiquity. The statement 'Vengeance is mine, saith the Lord' is in a strange way ambiguous. Though it ostensibly denies man the right to revenge, it simultaneously offers a kind of divine sanction to vengeance by providing a divine model of it. The God of the Old Testament is a vengeful God, and the God of the New, while offering forgiveness to sinners, raises the stakes involved in revenge by damning unrepentant sinners for all eternity. Hamlet's concern for the salvation of his soul makes him more thoughtful and hesitant than a classical hero, but it also means that if he is to take revenge on Claudius, it must be revenge on his immortal soul.

Shakespeare makes this literally the central issue of *Hamlet*. At roughly the middle of the play, at the traditional turning point of the five-act structure, Hamlet has an opportunity to kill Claudius. The king is alone, unguarded, and defenceless, and with the success of the play he stages, Hamlet is finally convinced that the ghost did tell the truth about the murder of his father. If he had killed Claudius at this moment, many if not all of the disasters which later occur might have been avoided. But he refuses to strike out against Claudius because of the situation in which he finds the king [i.e., in the midst of prayer]. . . .

At this crucial juncture, Hamlet's religious beliefs intervene to complicate his view of revenge in a peculiarly diabolical manner. He feels that he must act in such a way as to ensure, not just the destruction of Claudius's body, but the damnation of his soul. . . .

The task of vengeance becomes more complicated for a man who believes in the immortality of the soul. Some critics have pointed to the dramatic irony of Act III, scene iii. Claudius himself admits that his prayers have been ineffective; presumably, had Hamlet killed him at this moment, his soul would have gone to hell as the prince had hoped. But what critics who fault Hamlet for this reason do not acknowledge is that he has no way of knowing what we as the audience know. Unlike us, he does not hear Claudius's soliloquy: thus he has no reliable access to the King's inner feelings. . . . Since he can never have any objective evidence of whether the king's soul goes to heaven or to hell, everything comes to hinge on his ability to spy into Claudius's soul, which is to say, on his ability to interpret the state of his inner feelings. That Hamlet in fact misinterprets these feelings

A SUPERBLY SELF-CONTAINED CHARACTER

Just as Cantor singles out Horatio as having certain beliefs that contrast with Hamlet's, the noted nineteenth-century Shakespearean critic, H.N. Hudson, called attention to the differences between the two characters. Horatio, said Hudson, is able to keep a "calm, clear head" while his friend, the prince, agonizes.

Horatio is one of the very noblest and most beautiful of Shakespeare's characters; and there is not a single loose stitch in his make-up; he is at all times superbly self-contained; he feels deeply, but never gushes nor runs over; a most manly soul, full alike of strength, tenderness, and solidity. But he moves so quietly in the drama that his rare traits of character have hardly had justice done them. Should we undertake to go through the play without him, we might feel then how much of the best spirit and impression of the scenes is owing to his presence. He is the medium whereby many of the hero's finest and noblest qualities are conveyed to us, yet himself so clear and simple and transparent that he scarcely catches the attention. . . . The great charm of Horatio's unselfishness is that he seems not to be himself in the least aware of it; "as one, in suffering all, that suffers nothing." His mild scepticism at first, "touching this dreaded sight twice seen of us," is exceedingly graceful and scholarly. And indeed all that comes from him marks the presence of a calm, clear head, keeping touch and time perfectly with a good heart.

H.N. Hudson, "Introduction to Hamlet," quoted in Samuel Thurber and A.B. de Mille, eds., *Hamlet.* Boston: Allyn and Bacon, 1922, p. 181.

in Act III, scene iii is one indication of how his religious beliefs have introduced a new complexity into his possibilities for acting heroically.

HORATIO THE SKEPTIC

Fortunately, to raise the question of Hamlet's religious beliefs need not involve us in the thorny question of Shakespeare's. Though many critics have presumed to speak for Shakespeare on the issue of religion, it is extremely difficult —if not impossible—to construct a consistent religious doctrine out of his plays. But we can reasonably examine the religious sentiments which Shakespeare attributes to individual characters within his plays without thereby identifying these sentiments as Shakespeare's. Indeed, as a general point, what I have been trying to show is that Shakespeare characterizes his figures not simply in terms of what we might call their temperaments or personalities, but in terms of their opinions or beliefs or, more broadly, their views of the cosmos. We have seen that in considering basic questions about Hamlet such as: why does he not commit suicide or why does he not kill Claudius when he has the chance?, we must take into account his Christian belief in an afterlife. (Whether in the way he applies this belief Hamlet is behaving as a *good* Christian is very much open to dispute, but that his beliefs are those of a Christian as opposed to a pagan cannot be denied.) The complexity of Hamlet's stated view of the world—and above all the way it brings together classical and Christian elements in an uneasy fusion—may well be responsible for the fact that he cannot respond to the ghost's challenge in a simple and direct way.

Shakespeare's attention to the religious beliefs of his characters is evident in the care with which he differentiates them. For example, Horatio's distinctive set of beliefs helps to highlight Hamlet's. As his name indicates, there is something Roman about Horatio. This is, typically, most evident in his attitude towards suicide. When he tries to follow Hamlet in death, he explicitly views it as a pagan act: 'I am more an antique Roman than a Dane' (V.ii.341). When Hamlet discusses the qualities he admires in Horatio, he presents him in terms that call to mind a Roman Stoic (III.ii.63–74). Horatio's Romanness is related to a certain religious skepticism he displays. He is the one character to express doubts about the ghost:

> Horatio says 'tis but our fantasy,
> And will not let belief take hold of him.

> (I.i.23–4)

He refuses to take anything on hearsay and does not accept the fact of the ghost until he sees it with his own eyes (I.i.56–8). Even after experiencing the apparition, he refuses to give full assent to Marcellus's conventionally pious report of beliefs about ghosts; Horatio replies: 'So have I heard and do in part believe it' (I.i.165).

The fact that rational skepticism seems to be the keynote of Horatio's character may explain why Hamlet feels compelled to distinguish his philosophical position from his friend's:

> There are more things in heaven and earth, Horatio,
> Than are dreamt of in your philosophy. . . .

> (I.v.166–7)

DISGUSTED BY THE WORLD

Hamlet's metaphysical quarrel with Horatio gives an inkling of those aspects of his view of the world which work against his heroic impulses. Heroic action begins to lose some of its lustre when viewed from the perspective of eternity. For all his admiration for classical antiquity, Hamlet has a distinctly Christian sense of the transiency [impermanence] of the glory of the ancient world. He even sounds like a preacher in the way he imagines the nobility of Alexander the Great reduced to dust. . . . Hamlet measures the greatest of ancient heroes against the Christian standard of eternity and finds them wanting:

> Imperious Caesar, dead and turn'd to clay,
> Might stop a hole to keep the wind away. . . .

Related to Hamlet's concern with eternal as opposed to temporal things is a certain cosmopolitanism [worldliness] in his outlook. His mind is so wide-ranging and comprehensive that he finds it difficult to take Denmark and Danish affairs seriously. Though as a prince he ought to uphold the customs of his country, he in fact despises them. . . .

Hamlet's awareness of what other nations think of Denmark is in itself an admirable quality. His willingness to agree with foreign criticism of his countrymen shows the independence and integrity of his mind. But it also means that when Hamlet is called upon to purify Denmark, he will be less likely to believe that the task is worthwhile or even possible.

Shakespeare went out of his way to portray Denmark as a kind of cultural backwater in Europe. As *Hamlet* opens, both Laertes and Hamlet are asking permission to leave the country for more interesting locales, such as Paris and Wittenberg. One can get a measure of Hamlet's feeling for his native land by the fact that he tends to greet old friends with the question: 'What are you doing here?', with the implication 'when you could be somewhere more interesting'. The players who arrive at Claudius's court, far from rejoicing in an opportunity for a royal command performance, seem to view it as a kind of theatrical exile. Playing even at the court of Denmark apparently is regarded by the actors as being condemned to the provinces.

Hamlet is deeply disturbed by the provinciality of Denmark. He feels hemmed in, unable to give free rein to the expansive impulses of his spirit. But the problem is not simply with Denmark. . . . Hamlet has reason to believe that Denmark is particularly confining, but ultimately he feels imprisoned and disgusted by the world itself:

> How weary, stale, flat, and unprofitable
> Seem to me all the uses of this world!
>
> (I.ii.133–4)

Hamlet's *contemptus mundi* [world-hating] attitude is perhaps the most Christian aspect of his character and certainly the one most in tension with his admiration for classical heroism. Unlike a classical hero, he does not feel at home in this world. Far from believing that this world is all man has, he is haunted by visions of a world beyond.

HAMLET NO CLASSICAL HERO

Moreover, unlike a classical hero, Hamlet has a brooding sense that the appearances of this world conceal a deeper reality. That is why the world is so much more mysterious to him than it is to Achilles. . . . He lives in a world in which the truth seems covered by veil after veil, and in which men must resort to devious methods to spy it out. . . . Hamlet's disillusioning experiences— especially watching his mother betray the memory of his father—have led him to distrust appearances. Characteristically his first speech in the play expresses his contempt for seeming and his suspicion that truth lies buried beneath layers of deception (I.ii.76–86). His conviction that 'customary suits of solemn black' cannot express the truth of mourning reflects that general distrust of custom we saw in his attitude towards Denmark.

Hamlet is particularly disturbed by the customs of women, which call forth his most bitter and cynical remarks. Their habitual use of cosmetics symbolises for him the duplicity of the human world:

> I have heard of your paintings, well enough. God hath given you one face, and you make yourselves another.
>
> (III.i.142–4)

His obsession with women's makeup culminates in his instructions to Yorick's skull:

> Now get you to my lady's chamber, and tell her, let her paint an inch thick, to this favor she must come; make her laugh at that. . . .
>
> (V.i.192–5)

Faith in the heroic potentiality of humanity has a hard time withstanding this kind of questioning. To Hamlet a courtier is merely 'spacious in the possession of dirt'

(V.ii.87–8) and man himself, seemingly 'the beauty of the world; the paragon of animals', is reduced to a 'quintessence of dust' (II.ii.307-8).

Hamlet is thus characterised by a kind of absolutism. One can see this in the way he idealises the memory of his father into an image of perfection. . . . He has a kind of all-or-nothing attitude: if the world or people do not live up to his image of perfection, they are worthless to him. Thus, the more idealistic his view of heroism becomes, the less likely it is that any concrete act of heroism can satisfy him. . . .

Hamlet's doubts about heroism are chiefly focused on the inadequacy of the object to the heroic impulse. It is ironic, then, that the one time within the play when he strikes out with the impulsiveness of an epic hero, he does so in total ignorance of the object of his wrath. The way he murders Polonius—striking blindly through a curtain—is strangely emblematic [symbolic] of his whole situation. He is called upon to act heroically, but, unlike a classical hero, he is denied clear knowledge of the meaning of heroic action. When the elder Hamlet fought the elder Fortinbras, they stood face-to-face: each knew who his opponent was, and what they were fighting for. But in *Hamlet* everything happens, as it were, 'through a glass darkly'. . . . We tend to think of classical heroes fighting out their battles in broad daylight and in clear view of the public. But in *Hamlet*, much of the action takes place at night, deliberately hidden from public view, steeped in the deep secrecy of treachery.

Hamlet's doubts about the veracity of the ghost are only one example of the uncertainties which surround all his attempts at action. When he tries to act heroically in Act III, scene iv, he literally does not know what he is doing. The larger context of his action is obscure to him. In this sense, the murder of Polonius prefigures the final scene of the play, when Hamlet again can only blunder into acting heroically. . . . The prince finally accomplishes his revenge and dies in a profoundly ambiguous action: a game that is not really a game, a battle that is not really a battle, fighting against an opponent who is not his true opponent, in a cause that is not his true cause.

CHAPTER 4

Diverse Ways of Interpreting and Staging *Hamlet*

John Gielgud's Interpretation of *Hamlet* Sheds Light on the Play

Mary Z. Maher

University of Arizona scholar Mary Z. Maher here ably describes how British actor John Gielgud, widely seen as the "Hamlet of the century," interpreted and performed Hamlet's seven soliloquies. (Actually, Gielgud omitted the fifth soliloquy and so performed only six.) These great speeches are unquestionably among the most famous ever written; and one of them, the "To be, or not to be" speech, is probably *the* most famous. Gielgud first played Hamlet at London's Old Vic Theatre in 1929 and performed the role again in New York in 1936. In reconstructing the actor's motivations and vocal and physical approaches to the speeches, Maher draws on recollections by Shakespeare devotee Rosamond Gilder, who saw the 1936 production several times. According to Maher, who also personally interviewed Gielgud, the actor had seen several other performances of *Hamlet* before he played the role. These performances included those of the great nineteenth-century British actor, Sir Henry Irving, and popular stage and film actors John Barrymore and Leslie Howard. But in constructing his own interpretation, Gielgud tried not to copy these actors too directly. Ironically, his Hamlet turned out to be so great that many actors subsequently copied *him*.

Because of his extensive and varied experience with *Hamlet*, John Gielgud owned the role of the prince in a way that no other twentieth-century actor could. As [noted critic] James

Agate wrote of Gielgud's 1944 production, "Mr. Gielgud is now completely and authoritatively master of this tremendous part. He is, we feel, this generation's rightful tenant of this 'monstrous Gothic castle of a poem' . . . I hold that this is, and is likely to remain, the best Hamlet of our time." Gielgud played the role of Hamlet more than five hundred times in his long and distinguished career. He was one of the few modern actors who simultaneously performed in and directed himself as Hamlet. And in 1964 he was director of the play with yet another actor in the role, Richard Burton. . . .

Gielgud's view of the chief character, his mode of playing, and much of his stage business set the fashion for Hamlets in the decades to come. . . . In a 1988 television documentary titled "John Gielgud: An Actor's Life," the narrator said, "His memorable assumption of some roles has stamped an impression so deep that other actors have found it difficult to erase." As a model for others, Gielgud cannot be overestimated. Here, indeed, was a definitive Hamlet.

Gielgud came to the role steeped in its nuances and possessing an encyclopedic knowledge of past performances. A member of the famous theatrical family of Terrys, he "knew by heart the vivid description in Ellen Terry's memoirs of how [Henry] Irving played it." But when asked if he had modeled his performance after anyone, he replied,

> No, I didn't. I thought I had. I thought I would copy all the actors I'd ever seen, in turn, and by then I'd seen about a dozen or fifteen Hamlets. . . . Of course, Irving was my god, although I'd never seen him. . . . I didn't try to copy, I only took note of all the things he'd done and looked at the pictures of him and so on. But when it came to the Vic, the play moved so fast and there was so much of it that I suddenly felt, "Well, I've just got to be myself," and I really played it absolutely straight as far as I could. Of course, I was fortunate in that . . . Hamlet had never been allowed to be given to a very young actor until I played it. It was the kind of prize that an actor, when he went into management at the age of forty or fifty . . . allowed himself. . . .

NOBLE, BUT FULL OF FIRE

Gielgud played his first Hamlet in 1929, at the age of twenty-six, and his last in 1945. This essay will focus on his 1936 production because it was the best-documented. In that production, Gielgud's acting of the role was neither as melodramatic and passionate as Barrymore's, nor as bloodless and delicate as Leslie Howard's. Howard's *Hamlet* opened in

New York within a month of Gielgud's. The press created a "War of the Hamlets," thus generating publicity and box office sales for Gielgud's, which the critics preferred. Indeed, he was in top form for this second shot at it:

> The most thrilling Hamlet for me was the production in New York in 1936, because I felt I was on my mettle. It was my first big chance in America, and I was presented by an American management with an all-American cast. . . . Rehearsals were thrilling because everyone seemed so excited about my performance.

Critics reviewing the production spoke of his restraint from bellowing and ranting, his intellectualism, and his "modernizing" of the role, which appears to mean not only a simplicity and a spontaneity in the acting of it but also a retention of the doubleness of Hamlet's character. Gielgud kept the sardonic humor and the occasionally violent language; he remained noble, still very much the prince, yet he did not lack fire. Certainly, his performance choices suggest a volatile Hamlet. The play-within-the-play scene was unusually active: He actually held a manuscript (presumably the "dozen or sixteen lines" he asked the First Player to insert) and thumped out the meter of the lines as the players spoke. He also walked around during the performance of "The Mouse-trap," dropping pointed phrases into the ears of both king and queen. As the playlet closed, he leaped onto the king's empty throne, shouting triumphantly, waving the manuscript in the air and ultimately tearing it to tiny pieces, which he threw like confetti. He even took snuff from a silver box and then offered some to the gravedigger in that comic scene. The combination of melodramatic and realistic effects accounts for his being labeled both traditional and nontraditional. . . .

AN ANGUISHED FIRST SOLILOQUY

In the first "act" of the play (the production was divided into two acts, or nineteen scenes with one intermission), Gielgud was manic but never totally mad, and within the second half he presented an integrated personality who had come to terms with what he had to do. Gielgud mapped out certain "shocks," histrionic moments of realization, such as the Ghost's revelation of murder, which built to the firm resolution in the seventh soliloquy, "How all occasions do inform against me" (IV.iv.32–36).

Gielgud performed the first soliloquy ("O that this too too sallied flesh," I.ii.129–59), as if anguish were its chief tonal quality. It followed a court scene which was rendered intimate and domestic since the courtiers and attendants exited at I.i.63 once the official business concluded. Consequently, Hamlet's discussion with Claudius and Gertrude was decorously private, yet he clearly indicated that he disliked his uncle. After the king and queen exited, he began his soliloquy by making an important transition for the audience, effecting a change between the character's outer persona as presented to Gertrude and Claudius and the private self, who suffered from events. . . .

Gielgud continued the soliloquy by walking slowly upstage and coming to rest at the end of the council table. Finally, he turned and looked outward but did not make contact with the audience. On "weary, stale, flat, and unprofitable," each word dropped a note lower than the one before. As he began "so loving to my mother," the tempo accelerated as nausea about the recent marriage filled him. On the beat that ended "Let me not think on't," he covered his face with his hands. Unable to still his mind, he surged on obsessively: "a little month" began a build to the climax of "incestuous sheets." On the final two lines, he sank back "into apathy and hopeless sorrow." The soliloquy was delivered with two major vocal builds, some general slow movement about the set, and variety in emotion using horror and growing disgust as sizzling punctuation marks within a context of depression or "dull bitterness.". . .

Gielgud wrote about the first soliloquy as one of the most exciting for the actor because it "seem[ed] to set the character once and for all in the audience's minds." His actor's instincts told him that its position of primacy made it extremely important in establishing the audience-actor relationship. Once he had spoken, the actor could not make major changes in the character conception. Gielgud described the speech as a reaction to the first of a series of "shocks and surprises" that accumulate in the play. He felt that Hamlet, placed in an impossible predicament, found his way to his fate through episodes like this one. Since the actor spoke to himself (avoiding eye contact with individuals), he had no other need than to be truthful. The audience was eavesdropping on his agonies.

PHYSICAL COLLAPSE AND MENTAL CHAOS

The second soliloquy (at I.v.92–112) was clearly the second major shock in Hamlet's Denmark. It followed a very dramatic

THE DEEPER MAGIC OF IMAGINATION

Shakespearean scholar and critic E. Martin Brown, who attended all of Gielgud's productions of Hamlet, *describes how over time the great actor matured in the role.*

After three years in America, my first visit to an English theatre in 1930 introduced me to John Gielgud's Hamlet. . . .

His productions were simple—the Vic had very little money: but because they went for the essentials, simplicity proved a blessing. In this *Hamlet*, he gave to an actor of twenty-six . . . the chance to show himself, in a clear, unfussy production, as the greatest Hamlet of his age.

About the truth of that categorical statement I have no doubt. I have seen all the four English productions in which he played the part. People sometimes say that he never quite touched the original (1930) rendering: I believe that this is because they were seeing him in the part for the first time. Certainly the impact of that evening was unforgettable: and in seeing the subsequent productions I was never so swept away. But I had with Gielgud's Hamlet the experience which stamps a work of art as of supreme quality. At every seeing, new beauties revealed themselves: so that long after the magic of surprise was quite gone, the deeper magic of imagination went on working.

Two impressions remain most vividly from 1930. First, the youth of the Prince. My first Hamlet was sixty when I saw him. Gielgud is four years younger than I am: and though I had always loved the play so deeply, I had never felt it speak so piercingly to myself from the stage. It was not that his youthfulness was pathetic, but that it accentuated his loneliness and the difficulty of coping with a world of older people: and the mother-son relationship . . . was made startlingly real. The other new impression was of wormwood—the iron that had entered into Hamlet's soul. A sensitive young man had suddenly seen the ugliness that can be found in human life: it nauseated and embittered him.

This was not a 'sympathetic' Hamlet, but a character at once forceful and poetic. Gielgud balanced the two elements to make his Hamlet a person, as the performance matured through the three subsequent productions of 1934, 1936 and 1944. The later performances became a little more deliberate; perhaps by producing the play himself he inevitably lost some of the spontaneity of 1930, but this was off-set by a gain in dignity and in the profound understanding of the reflective passages in particular.

"English Hamlets of the Twentieth Century," in Allardyce Nicoll, ed., *Shakespeare Survey*. Cambridge, Eng.: Cambridge University Press, 1956.

appearance by the Ghost, which ended with Hamlet's body lying on the ground racked with sobs. [Witness Rosamond] Gilder described the atmosphere: "The quick step and harsh quick words are the outward sign of all that has been growing in him since he heard of the Ghost, the tension that rises steadily, notch by notch, like a tightened violin string till it cracks at the Ghost's departure."

Gielgud was aided by scenic effects here. The stage was darkened, and there was the eerie sound of wind blowing as Hamlet appeared on the ramparts. After the exchange between Ghost and son, Gielgud fell to his knees, his hand extended to the departing creature as lights blacked out for a hushed pause. Soon lights came up again faintly, and the soliloquy began with an "animal wail of pain":

> He turns on himself, self-lacerating, driving unpityingly . . . little by little, he raises himself on one knee. He is bruised, beaten; only his will remains and forces him up, governing even the "distracted globe" which is indeed overburdened to the verge of frenzy.

> "Ay, thou poor ghost" brings again the note of tenderness and pity, pity for the dead and for his father in his torment. The second "Remember thee" is an oath. The words that follow come quickly, rising in a swift crescendo of dedication to the final "yes, by heaven" which brings him to his feet. A pause, and then the infamy sweeps over him. "O most pernicious woman!" His first thought, even before Claudius and murder, is of her. Then his mind turns to Claudius—to the morning scene of flattery and smug smiles, to the laughter and revelry below at this very moment. His voice breaks with anger at such villainy. He moves to the right, almost to the spot where the Ghost had stood. On the tablet from which he has just wiped all "trivial fond records," on his brain seared by the Ghost's revelations, he will register this shame. The phrase ends on a high, hard challenge: "So, uncle, there you are," as he strikes his forehead with his hand.

> Then, deep and very quiet, the oath of consecration, "Now to my word." Both hands clasp the sword-hilt. The blade gleams in an arc as he raises it to his lips. He stands straight as a lance, the silver line above his head piercing heavenward in salute. Slowly, with finality, with full and weary prescience, he lowers the sword, "I have sworn 't."

Gilder's description of the soliloquy and her use of the word "frenzy" indicates that Gielgud enacted a total collapse, a physical shattering as well as mental chaos. The soliloquy was as personal as a nervous breakdown. It was therefore not shared with the theatre audience. He was deeply shaken but managed to restore his equilibrium through the ritual resolve of the final vow. . . .

LIKE "ONE LOOSED OUT OF HELL"

For the third soliloquy ("O, what a rogue and peasant slave am I!" II.ii.550–605), Gielgud followed a through-line of action which began in the previous scene with the players. . . . After the Hecuba speech, he took a very long pause to study the player's face as if he saw within the man a reflection of his own dilemma. This set the audience up for the forthcoming comparison of the player's emotions to Hamlet's emotions, a major propellant in the thrust of the third soliloquy. Hamlet reprimanded Polonius in telling him how to treat the players, making his rebuke an "explosion" rather than advice, since tension had mounted under his skin during the player's speech. All of the players exited, and Hamlet drew one of them aside to ask for some "dozen or sixteen lines" to be inserted into the Gonzago play.

Then followed a piece of business which helped Gielgud make the transition into the soliloquy. Rosencrantz and Guildenstern remained onstage to continue talking with Hamlet; however, "with a swift, repelling gesture, he dismisses them." He then took a long pause, his back turned to the audience, and leaned on his hands on the table. This gesture endowed the first line "Now I am alone," with special meaning: in his desolation, he shared his anguish with no one. This also gave him preparation time for the burst of bottled anger that launched the whole first section of the soliloquy.

"O, what a rogue" began a torrent of self-deprecation, and Gielgud continued a vocal build to "damn'd defeat was made," whereupon he fell on a stool. But the battering of self had not stopped. He plunged into the short questions with vehement speed, rising quickly on "Who does me this?" There was a third build; this time his body shook with anger, the pitch of his voice rose up on "treacherous, *lecherous kindless villain!*" On the famous climactic "Oh Vengeance!" he grabbed his dagger and smashed it into the doorway; the dagger fell from his raised arm, and his body melted onto the top step with a pitiful bleat, "Fie upon it! Foh!" A long pause ensued in which only sobbing could be heard.

Finally, there was a slow movement: he raised his head tentatively on "About, my brains." Soon an idea was seen registering on his face, his voice hoarse and whispery. Once he had begun, the details of the plan were important and accumulated quickly. Gielgud added to this speed a bit of madness: "the look of one loosed out of hell." He took a long pause before the final two lines in order to consider once more whether he was led by the devil or an honest ghost; his plan would ensure "grounds more relative." The scene closed with feverish business: "Gielgud throws himself into a chair beside the table and begins to write wildly on a piece of paper. There is a blackout."

Gielgud divided the soliloquy into two distinct performance beats. The first half built to near-climax and a culminating peak at "Oh Vengeance!" Then followed six lines of transition, with Gielgud on his knees. The second section, played downstage and closer to the audience, was about plotting, where Hamlet posed the play-within-the-play solution. The business at the end, scribbling wildly, was an idea borrowed from Irving, an epilogue in which the actor begged for favor. For Gielgud confessed that early on in his career, he felt the final couplet should provide the logical moment for the greatest applause in the play. . . .

EXAMINING THE VOID

The fourth soliloquy ("To be, or not to be," III.i.55–89) followed a mere fifty-five lines later. The scene was in the great hall of the castle, a huge room with two flights of stairs. The business of stowing Ophelia had been dispatched by Polonius and Claudius. Hamlet came in defiantly, stage right. He saw that no one was there and continued to the stage left platform, where he began the famous lines thoughtfully and inwardly; there was no attempt to speak to the audience. Gielgud reported that it was occasionally difficult to ignore them because "frequently one can hear words and phrases being whispered by people in the front rows, just before one is going to speak them."

This soliloquy was clearly more cerebral than the others; Gilder calls it "mystic contemplation." She recounts that each successive idea registered on Gielgud's face as Hamlet mentally shuffled the thoughts for consideration. The possibility and the longing toward death were balanced against the fear of what it means to no longer be alive. He seemed to be moving toward one concept particularly, a mind magnetized by the need to examine the void: perhaps it was like sleeping; perhaps it was like sleeping *no more*, and so Gielgud emphasized those words.

Gielgud used few gestures and little movement in delivering the speech. On "bare bodkin," he omitted the actual knife but suggested it with a pantomimic movement of the left hand, as though a dagger lay point inward in his palm. On the phrase "puzzles the will," he began to pace about the stage. His restless movement at this juncture indicated that he had returned from his trance to the world of action. He needed to get on with the task. Ophelia entered, and the spell of the speech was broken.

Gielgud carefully connected this speech with the big soliloquy which preceded it: "I now realize that the effect of despondency in 'To be, or not to be' is a natural and brilliant psychological reaction from the violent and hopeless rage of the earlier speech." Closely juxtaposed as they are, the two soliloquies provide differing but perfectly legitimate responses for a passionate and intelligent man: "Rogue and peasant slave" effectively purges, and "To be" theorizes, philosophizes, contemplates. Gielgud also noted that "various directors have changed the order of the scenes and placed the two soliloquies in an exchanged sequence. I can see no excuse for this theory.". . .

Both the third and the fourth soliloquies end in irresolution toward carrying out the deed. This Hamlet wanted resolution or he would not have chastised himself so caustically during the third soliloquy. "To be" showed that he had serious cause to consider the weighty consequences: once Hamlet decides to act, many people's lives are irrevocably altered. . . .

THE FIFTH AND SIXTH SOLILOQUIES

The fifth soliloquy ("'Tis now the very witching time of night," III.ii.388–99) was omitted entirely. . . .

Gielgud's choice to cut the fifth soliloquy is defensible from a theatrical point of view. . . . Here, he chose to include business [physical gestures and bits] that was part of the performance tradition of *Hamlet*. Second, to deliver the soliloquy might have destroyed the moment in a scene that was carefully designed to reach a theatrical peak. Finally, the major point of the soliloquy, Hamlet's intention to "do such bitter business as the day / Would quake to look on" had been aptly made without speaking those lines. The actor had made a performance choice—to act the intention of the lines rather than to say them. In a production where very few textual cuts were made, this one was perhaps justifiable.

The sixth soliloquy ("Now might I do it pat," III.iii.73–96) took place in Claudius' "dressing room." Preparation for the scene was very intricate. . . . As the king knelt to pray, he heard a noise, so he got up and swung the drapery back with his sword. Seeing nothing amiss, he laid the sword on the chair, and returned to his praying. The audience was now fully anticipating an intruder, and when the drapery next shivered, Hamlet appeared and approached only so far as the chair, which he grasped. He saw the sword and announced, "Now might I do it pat," as he snatched it and pulled his sword arm back to strike. All of this took place behind and out of sight of the king. As Hamlet spoke, the mental image of sending Claudius to heaven while his father's shade wandered in hell arrested his sword. On "Up, sword," he cradled the long blade in his left arm and "crouching forward he pours out the venomous words, enunciating the plan he determines to carry out: then with a swift stealthy swing he is at the doorway again. One last glance, a flash, and he is gone." The king looked up quickly at his empty chair, sensing a narrow escape as he saw that the sword had disappeared entirely and then heard Hamlet's cry to Gertrude offstage. It was one brief, illumined movement for Gielgud: an appearance, a quick judgment, a retreat—certainly not a moment for contemplation.

Gielgud was proud of the stage business with the sword, partly because he considered it to be his own invention. . . . Furthermore, he felt that in his production, as well as in most productions, the prayer scene stretched truth extraordinarily. Like the fifth soliloquy, this speech "is one that does not go with an audience." Unless an elaborate staging plan was used to physically separate Claudius and Hamlet, the audience would simply not believe that the two characters could not overhear one another's soliloquies.

A NEW SENSE OF PURPOSE

The last soliloquy ("How all occasions do inform against me," IV.iv.32–66) is described by Gilder thus:

> Scene 13. A plain in Denmark.
> A backdrop suggests a barren stretch of plain with gnarled trees breaking the grey expanse. Fortinbras talks with one of his captains and there is a sound of martial music in the distance. As the two soldiers are leaving, right, Hamlet comes in from the opposite side with Rosencrantz, Guildenstern and an attendant. He recalls the captain for a moment's colloquy on the subject of Fortinbras' expedition against Poland. The

spectacle of this army of men ready to do battle, to die, for a "straw" arrests his attention. Shading his eyes with his hand he looks out toward the distant encampment. For a long moment he stands lost in thought and then dismisses the soldier. A word from Rosencrantz reminds him of the presence of his associates—and he sends them on ahead remaining alone in contemplation of his obsessing problem; thought and action in eternal conflict.

There was a distinct change of tone in the delivery of this soliloquy, which Gilder describes as "an inner assurance." The self-deprecation was still present but seemed somehow more clear-eyed, more in perspective. The acting reflected this: "His tone is firm, the timbre of his voice strong and resonant, his few gestures clear-cut, decisive."

As Hamlet described Fortinbras, he compared himself with the Norwegian prince. Fortinbras would endanger others' lives for a straw, an eggshell: one's motivations need not be over-justified if honor is the issue. Gielgud's Hamlet drew strength from the image of soldiers plunging to their deaths, and his eyes and face shone with rededication, his voice vibrated with purpose.... Now he saw an opportunity and embraced it. Gielgud viewed "How all occasions" as a "very *important* soliloquy" that showed Hamlet's state of mind as "clear, noble, and resolved" before he went to England, with a "clear understanding of his destiny and desire." Here was an assertion of the Victorian notion of the noble prince who valued honor above "the death of twenty thousand men." After World War II and Vietnam, it would become less and less popular to find inspiration in Fortinbras, and, in fact, his portrayal on the stage would become more and more brutal and dictatorial.

PSYCHOLOGICAL REALISM

Most of Gielgud's discussions of the soliloquies are rendered from the point of view of what must have been going on in Hamlet's mind as Hamlet *talked with his inner self.* . . . Consequently, Hamlet was his own audience, and the theatre audience was in the position of overhearing very personal matters. The actor never violated decorum nor attempted to interact with the audience. In turn, the spectators did not become his sounding board or his support system. This self-communing Hamlet reflected the twentieth-century pre-occupation with psychological realism. The performance choice to speak the soliloquies inwardly was consistent with the ideas of the decade. . . .

Gielgud strongly advised that "the soliloquy is most easily spoken close to the footlights," "always as far downstage as possible"—references to that trough of lights so often present in proscenium arch theatres. A Hamlet would have been deterred from addressing the theatre audience because the lights in his eyes would have prevented him from seeing them and thus would have worked to separate actor and audience. We can rest assured that this actor would have made eyes and face visible and available to the audience, and he also would have been distinctly and precisely tuned to stirrings and responses from them. However, he never described himself as the ultimate sharer with the audience nor did he make specific efforts to contact them.

The inward soliloquy elicited a certain kind of performance from the actor. In this production, Gielgud's movements were large, flowing, and melodramatic. . . . If the actor does not step forward onto the apron and "say" his feelings to an audience, i.e., articulate the depth of his emotions directly, then he can be granted license to more broadly *en*-act them, to increase the physical size and scope of his performance. Stepping forward to address the audience is a step nearer to bringing the camera in closer; it is the stage analogue of a close-up shot. And stepping back from the camera (from the audience) allows the actor larger physical manifestations of his inner emotion. . . .

It was of major importance that Gielgud's soliloquies were not delivered using direct eye contact with the audience. This tradition remained strong in the theatre up through the middle of the twentieth century. Although Gielgud did not set the fashion, and although his presentation did not take place on a "realistic set," his model was enormously influential in perpetuating the tradition of performing the world's most famous speeches during the first half of the twentieth century, a period when the basic actor-audience relationship in theatre structures was changing. It was not until the sixties that other actors began to experiment with the performance mode of the soliloquies within theatre spaces. Gielgud truly was "the glass of fashion and the mould of form" through which modern Hamlets mirrored themselves.

An Actor's Interpretation of *Hamlet*

Laurence Olivier

Laurence Olivier, who died in 1989, has been
dubbed by most dramatic critics and other actors as
"the greatest actor of the century." As a performer,
his physical and vocal range and emotional depth
were enormous and he was known for his bravura,
larger-than-life portrayals, especially of great Shakespearean characters. In this excerpt from his 1986
book, *On Acting*, he recalls searching, when still a
young man, for motivations and meaning in the
enigmatic, convoluted, and difficult role of Hamlet.
First, he takes us back to his initial assault on the
character—the 1937 London production directed by
the legendary theatrical producer-director, Tyrone
Guthrie. It was in preparing for this production that
Olivier learned about the "Freudian" idea that Hamlet harbors repressed sexual feelings for his own
mother, a notion then being promoted by Freud's fol-
lower, Ernest Jones. Olivier then recollects attempting to answer other questions about the character: Is
he a pacifist? Is he a coward? Did he sleep with
Ophelia? Finally, in telling about a spontaneously
improvised performance of the play at Elsinore, in
Denmark, Olivier suggests that when actors are put
on the spot, they can find meanings they never knew
existed in a role.

Hamlet is pound for pound, in my opinion, the greatest play
ever written. It towers above everything else in dramatic literature. It gives us great climaxes, shadows and shades, yet
contains occasional moments of high comedy. Every time
you read a line it can be a new discovery. You can play it and

Reprinted from *On Acting*, by Laurence Olivier (London: Weidenfeld & Nicolson,
1986), by permission of Orion Publishing Group, Ltd. Copyright 1986 by Wheelshare
Ltd.

play it as many times as the opportunity occurs and still not get to the bottom of its box of wonders. It can trick you round false corners and into culs-de-sac, or take you by the seat of your pants and hurl you across the stars. It can give you moments of unknown joy, or cast you into the depths of despair. Once you have played it, it will devour you and obsess you for the rest of your life. It has me. I think each day about it. I'll never play him again, of course, but by God, I wish I could.

HAMLET SUFFERING FROM AN OEDIPUS COMPLEX?

The first time I was going to play the part, at the Old Vic, I felt that it was crucial to establish that Hamlet was bone-real from the very first word. I was determined to take the audience with me, to make them believe that this man lived. I knew that earlier players of this part had thought that Hamlet should begin on a strange note, but I decided it would be kindest to my audience to keep it simple, not to frighten them to death with the high theatricality of my opening.

Whenever an actor first attempts Hamlet, he should be aware that it's a sporadic collection of self-dramatizations in which he tries always to play the hero and, in truth, feels ill cast in the part. His imagination is working as though he were a hero, but his soul is working in the brave light of the author, who decided to write a play with a hero who wasn't a hero. Witness the soliloquy "How all occasions . . ." following hard upon his staring enviously at Fortinbras, the ideal man of the times.

Many years ago, when I was first to play Hamlet at the Old Vic, I went with Tyrone Guthrie, who was going to direct it, and Peggy Ashcroft, who was going to play Ophelia (but for some regrettable reason wasn't able to), to see Professor Ernest Jones, the great psychiatrist, who had made an exhaustive study of Hamlet from his own professional point of view and was wonderfully enlightening. His book on the subject was called *What Happens in Hamlet*.

We talked and talked. He believed that Hamlet was a prime sufferer from the Oedipus complex. There are many signals along the line to show his inner involvement with his mother. One of them is his excessive devotion to his father. Nobody's that fond of his father unless he feels guilty about his mother, however subconscious that guilt may be. Hamlet's worship of his father is manufactured, assumed; he needs it to cover up his subconscious guilt. The Oedipus complex may, indeed, be responsible for a formidable share of all that is wrong with Hamlet. I myself am only too happy to allow to be added to Shakespeare's other acknowledged gifts an intuitive understanding of psychology. Why not? He was the world's greatest man. . . .

I can't remember if Jones came to see the production; I don't think he did. But I warned him that he would not find the Oedipal theory overt, though, of course, it would be there. He said, "I wouldn't suggest you should make it overt, as long as you know about it. That's the important point. You're not supposed to tell the audience with every wink and nod that one of the reasons for your present predicament is that you wish you were still hanging on your mother's tits." A very entertaining man.

THE FIRST PACIFIST?

Speaking of finding new meanings in the text, its forever being fresh, I thought of one the other day. In the grave scene when Laertes is mourning Ophelia and the unknown figure announces, "This is I, Hamlet the Dane," I believe he is saying, "I am King"—echoes of his father, whom he must have heard at some time saying this in anger, maybe on a number of occasions. When I was playing it, I just thought the outburst was merely another show of temperament, another side of his self-expression. But no, he had to find other people to be all the time, and it didn't occur to me that at this moment it was his father. The audience wouldn't have known for a second what I was at, but it would have helped me greatly. There can be found a slight hint of it, but a sweetly tender one, during the duel with Laertes, when his mother drinks the poison obviously intended for Hamlet.

Hamlet's continual complaining throughout the play is expressed directly to the audience, and he says almost in as many words no less than twice, "It's no good; I can't do it, can I? I wish I knew why. Am I a coward? Who dares pluck my beard? Am I this? Am I that? It's no good; I can't." Many people read into that the first pacifist; indeed, some remark that he's the first hero any author dared create from a hero who was no hero at all. But there are others, and I think this makes a marvelously firm argument for his Oedipus complex, who say he can kill his uncle/father when he is behind the arras, because he can say to himself he didn't know it was he . . . alas, poor Polonius. It is *after it is done* that he shouts victoriously to his mother, "Is it the King?" in the desperate hope he has done it without knowing it. He would rather act a part than do it: rather stab through a curtain than stab the King.

When Laertes has knifed him and death is a few breaths away, he is suddenly free to wreak vengeance because he has the innocent, pure reason of vengeance for himself, not for his guilt over his mother. Once he realizes he is about to touch hands with death, he is free, his guilt is expunged by his own murder, and he is able to feel, "You murder me and I'll murder you." For me that makes a final keystone in the arch of the argument for the Oedipus complex.

THE MAN IN BLACK

Though I believe this theory, I do not believe it to the extent of letting the play be just about that. The play is about a character who has that particular eccentricity, that particular thing *in* his character. When one thinks of audience after audience for nearly four hundred years trying to work it out, it is fascinating. Shakespeare was simply pouring out all that was in his instinctive heart at the time; it is an extraordinary exploration into the human mind.

"The man in black" is always interesting; as an actor your job is to enable the audience to follow his journey from one characteristic to another, from mood to mood. The actor must be absolutely clear in his mind where he is going, whatever theories he has nursed (and over the years there have been many); in the end he must tell the story.

But the questions keep on coming up, and always will. Was Hamlet this? Was he that? Did he do this, did he do that? *Did he sleep with Ophelia?* In reply to this last, one old actor-manager, early in the century, said, "In *my* company, *always!*" As far as I'm concerned there was nothing platonic in the relationship: when it's played as brother and sister I have no time for it. Hamlet is not just imagining what is beneath Ophelia's skirts; he has found out for himself—"country matters"—for certain. "Get thee to a nunnery! Why wouldst thou be a breeder of sinners?" Ophelia's problem is that she truly believes that the four-poster will become permanent and legal, and that she will eventually wear the crown of Denmark. Hamlet's problem is that he wants to follow his mother to the bedchamber as well . . . and does? Most un-

OLIVIER'S FAMOUS FILM VERSION

Noted film critic and scholar Roger Manvell here briefly recounts how Olivier used the "close-up" medium of film to extract motivations and meanings from the title character and story that would have been impossible in a stage production.

Those of Hamlet's soliloquies which are retained [by Olivier in the film] are treated as a mixture of voiced thought and direct speech. For example, the speech, 'O! that this too too solid flesh would melt', begins with Hamlet's expressions responding to the significance of the words which are heard spoken on the sound track as he wanders thoughtfully in the empty hall, finally going up to the King's throne-chair and leaning on it; only with the words, '—and yet, within a month—' do his lips move in direct speech. In the later soliloquy, 'To be or not to be', music and the natural sounds of the sea provide a backing to the spoken thought—direct speech only coming suddenly into play with the words, 'perchance to dream'. . . .

The acting is full of detailed touches, similar to those of Hamlet's reaction, throughout. The light-haired wig used by the boy-player in the travelling company suddenly reminds Hamlet of Ophelia's blonde hair; the scene with Yorick's skull becomes peculiarly moving because the skull, seen in close-shot, becomes like a real person—an effect all but impossible to achieve on the stage. Ophelia's child-like behaviour with Laertes, obviously a much-admired elder brother, reveals early on her extreme youth, and her utter incapacity to act with independent judgment when she is exploited later on by her elders in their conspiracy against Hamlet. In contrast to these often delicate points of detail is the bravura of performance so dear to Laurence Olivier, revealing him to be a theatrical showman as well as a great artist. The duel scene, lasting ten minutes and taking fourteen days to shoot, is magnificently intense, with the growing rage of the contestants. The melodramatic flying leap down from a height onto Claudius, when Hamlet plunges his sword into his uncle's body at the end of the play, is in tune with similar effects practised in the theatre—for example, in the production of *Coriolanus* at Stratford-upon-Avon in 1959; Olivier was at one stage hung upside down, grasped by the ankles. The jump [in the *Hamlet* film] was sufficiently dangerous to be made the final shot in the production.

Roger Manvell, *Shakespeare and the Film.* London: Debt, 1971, pp. 42–43.

likely—but the Gertrude/Hamlet scene in the first production I did at the Old Vic went about as far in this direction as I dared suggest, or the Ghost's complaints would have been on a different score.

LIKE A FAVORITE TEDDY BEAR

I had always decided that if I ever had the chance to lead a company I would start off with the big one, and in 1937 the chance came and I did. Of course, I was still not forgiven by a lot of the critics for my verse speaking, and there were still odious comparisons, as I suppose there always have to be. It may be that the young actor today has to suffer because my shadow has been left upon certain roles; not that I'm objecting, now, you understand. In those days [John] Gielgud was the top dog when it came to verse speaking and his Hamlet was very popular, with me as with the majority of theatergoers.

I was determined to win through, and in the end, I think I did. But perhaps that's not for me to say. Truth . . . speak the truth, though the verse will not entirely take care of itself. Shakespeare knew what he was doing; he put the rhythms there and he didn't wish them to be ignored.

Looking back now, forty-eight years later, I find it difficult to see that performance with absolute clarity, though there is still a warmth that remains with me. People who have never experienced that walk between one wing and another will probably wonder what I mean by warmth. It gets into the nostrils and into the hair; it is a combination of electric light, glue, rancid paint and scent. It is like a favorite Teddy bear, or stepping from an airplane into the warm sun. Once experienced, it stays forever, calling the actor back again and again, like a siren's song. . . .

Whatever people may have thought of my Hamlet, I think it was not bad. I know it was not perfection, but it *was* mine. I did it. It was *mine.*

My film interpretation of Hamlet was also all mine. I still think, after all these years, that the film stands up, much cut though it had to be, and I am still proud of it. A film can never show you what the actor was really like on the stage, but it can give you a very clear idea, and I have grown most wantonly partial to that medium. Its powers are apparently limitless.

Like any great play, *Hamlet* is totally adaptable. By this I mean it can be performed anywhere with anything. It can have a set, it can be played against drapes, it can be done before a brick wall. It lends itself to "the corner of the room.". . .

"WERE YOU THERE THAT NIGHT?"

I think one of the best performances I was involved in was probably at Elsinore in Denmark. Pouring, drenching rain meant that we could not open outside as we had intended to, and consequently, after a hurried discussion, it was decided that we would perform in the ballroom, which meant a rapid restaging. Tony (Tyrone) Guthrie, our director, was busy organizing things for the real opening, and something had to be arranged about seating for future performances, so he was heavily involved in administration. He left it to me to set it up and rehearse the new moves around the strange area that was now to accommodate us. As he went off, he said, "Fix it for me, Larry. Just place it all as you think best." So I did. All the movements had to be changed, so all the lovely invention was left to me. As you can imagine, I was thrilled to do it and, of course, enjoyed myself wildly.

There is nothing better than a group of actors being presented with a problem of this kind and having to improvise. When time is drifting away and the performance is getting closer, somehow the release of adrenaline creates an excitement that runs through everyone, from the leading actor/actress to the maker of the tea. The entire company pulls together with the one object in mind. It is at such times that you can ask for the impossible, and get it. "I'm afraid the only way you can play this scene is by hanging from the chandelier, dear boy." Without a moment's hesitation, the reply would come back, "Of course—no problem.". . .

Somehow every performance seems to be enhanced in times of unexpected difficulties; there is an edge, a fine edge that hoists the players, even the least inspired, onto another level. All the actors' motors have to be running, but in a low gear for greater acceleration. Nobody dares get a moment wrong. Whereas laziness, even boredom, may have crept in before—and this is very understandable when you think in terms of standing night after night on the end of a spear with somebody else delivering the dialogue that you feel you could do better—that boredom, for a moment, is forgotten and the contribution becomes genuine, energetic and electric. Everyone becomes a Thoroughbred, muscles alive and alert. The vibrations are high, and this will affect the audience as well. What they witness will be a night that they will always remember. "Were you there that night at Elsinore? I was." It is amazing how many people now think they were there. . . .

Whether or not what the audience sees is good we will never know, but the energy that is directed towards them will engulf them in its euphoric state. In Elsinore that night, the actors were heroes, every man Jack of them. I know—I was right in the middle of it. A dignity and excitement was achieved, an atmosphere in which no one falls on his arse unless it is intended. Everyone thrills with a sense of achievement and importance—and quite rightly. The "one for all" society syndrome. Above all, the performance was spontaneous.

I remember giving the stage at one moment to Torin Thatcher; he was playing the Ghost. We had erected a little stage for the play scenes and stuff, with some stairs that led up to it. I knelt by the stairs, facing away from the audience, and when, as the Ghost, he turned at the top, he found himself in this glorious solo upstage position. It was magnificent. I remember remarking to Tony Guthrie, "Wasn't it heavenly when Torin found himself so placed for his big scene with me?" and Tony replied, "Yes, it flowed through the ballroom like warm strawberry jam." I took that as a compliment.

It is a great night to remember, full of magic and memories. Some say it was the best thing they'd ever seen. Whether it was or not I'll never know, but it must have been something special. It rained, and because of this, the gods came over to our side. I think they always do, if handled with respect.

A DROP IN THE OCEAN

Enough has been said about Hamlet by others with better literary qualifications than mine; all I know is that he has a myriad of hidden problems you can never quite explain. He is utterly unlike Coriolanus [the title character in Shakespeare's play about the early Roman Republic], who is absolutely straightforward, with nothing of particular psychological interest. Coriolanus is himself; he knows it, his mother knows it. I can tell you how I crept inside him, inside Othello or Richard [the title character of Shakespeare's *Richard III*]; but I cannot tell you how I crept inside Hamlet, the man. Hamlet just takes you by the hand and either treats you roughly or shows you the way to the stars. All I know is he captured me, and once he had, he never let me go.

Scholars have not stopped theorizing about *Hamlet* since the day that [Shakespeare's friend, Richard] Burbage played its first performance. So what I feel about it, though important to me, is probably no more than a drop in the ocean so far as the academics are concerned, but it does have the special authority of the practitioner.

I suppose it must have been performed more times than any other play in the English language, with every performance at least slightly different, which is fascinating to think on. It is, without a doubt, the best play ever written, partly perhaps because it lends itself to so many changes and interpretations. The actor, however he plays it, well or badly, will get something right in his journey from the castle walls to his final silence.

I could see it and read it forever. Yes, the best play in the world.

A Television Interpretation of *Hamlet*

Bernice W. Kliman

Hamlet has been performed in a wide variety of
stage and film settings and directors have often attempted to use these visual trappings to enhance the
dramatic impact of their productions. One such attempt took place in 1964, when director Philip
Saville shot a TV production of the play, starring the
popular stage and film actor, Christopher Plummer,
on location at Kronborg Castle in Elsinore, Denmark.
This essay is a detailed critique of the film by Bernice W. Kliman, cofounder of the *Shakespeare on
Film Newsletter* and prolific writer about Shakespeare's works. According to Kliman, Saville hoped
that the authentic location would add atmosphere to
his production and allow him to make visual statements about many of the lines and characters that
would be more difficult to achieve in a live stage
show. However, says Kliman, while Plummer's performance as the Danish prince was outstanding, the
results of the location shooting did not live up to expectations. Because of the manner in which Saville
chose to stage the scenes and his overuse of camera
close-ups, the real castle settings were not utilized to
their best advantage. This ultimately detracted from
rather than intensified the power of the lines and
underscores the importance of matching style with
setting when staging the play.

Stage productions have foundered at Elsinore, battling poor
acoustics and rain, but a television production can overcome
these impediments with electronics and patience. For this
production, an article in *Newsweek* tells us, technicians

Reprinted from "Hamlet": *Film, Television, and Audio Performance*, by Bernice W. Kliman (Rutherford, NJ: Fairleigh Dickinson University Press, 1988), by permission of
Associated University Presses. Copyright 1988 by Bernice W. Kliman.

learned to shoot sequences between the twenty-four-second intervals of an incessant foghorn. But the possible is not always the advantageous, for the architectural drama of Elsinore does not necessarily enhance the drama of *Hamlet.*

Interestingly enough, perhaps because of the small size of the British and Danish home screen in 1963, the shooting style remains like that of the studio, emphasizing closeups, usually ignoring the setting. And indeed, sometimes the setting is not suitable. . . . Even a made-up castle in the studio can have a more profound effect on the viewer's senses than Elsinore's elegant reality, which is both less and more than one wants.

WORKING TOO HARD TO CREATE DRAMA

The film tries to badger the viewer into seeing what the setting lacks: a title says, "On a Promontory on the Sound Leading to the Baltic Sea Stands a Fortified Palace Symbolic of the Power of the King of Denmark." The word "promontory" notwithstanding, there is no high point at the coast of Elsinore, a flat and unprepossessing shore. The filmmakers have to use some sleight of hand with the camera to give the effect they are seeking. Very low-angle shots of the surf look as if the camera has been dug into the sand to get a crab's-eye view of the beach. Even from this angle, with a little softening through out-of-focusing, with a cooperative surf, and with rugged wave sounds coupled with danger music, with light glowing on the foam in general darkness, the shore looks inviting rather than foreboding. For the third scene of the Plummer version, the camera shows a small boat at quayside, Laertes and Ophelia at the shore, with the castle in the background. This daylight shot reveals all too plainly how level the sea coast is. If the setting had been . . . more dramatic in itself, the director would not have had to work so hard to create drama. Or, as in the [1964 John] Gielgud production, he could have used acting alone to suggest the danger and menace of Elsinore.

For the high promontory where Marcellus, Bernardo, and Horatio react to the ghost, a beach wall perhaps only inches high must do, but again, the extreme low angle of the shots, tilted upwards from ground level, tries to give an effect of height and distance to what is actually flat and close. These shots are coupled with overhead shots, as from the ghost's perspective, so that we never get an ordinary, straight-on shot of the three men, whom we see only one at a time. The film avoids giving a sense of the whole. Wind and surf sounds do not add as much as they might have if the setting had been more compelling. Perhaps because the setting is not satisfactory, the first scene is cut to a mere three lines, taking less than a minute of film time. We see the ghost neither here nor in the later scenes.

The director apparently meant to substitute the subsequent visual effect for the dialogue of scene one. A bridge between exterior and interior added to Shakespeare's script and entitled "Kronborg Castle" introduces a view of the castle. With the continued threatening music of both titles and first scene, a high-angle tilt shot through a row of columns shows a line of soldiers, marching across the courtyard below. A cut to the roof reveals another line of soldiers, partisans in their hands, standing guard. Seeing them, one wonders why the first scene did not take place on the roof, which might have felt dangerous. Perhaps it was thought that the proximity to the sea, with its wind-whipped sea-grass, gave the first scene more atmosphere. A cut to the inside and we see in a boot-level shot the soldiers marching through—as we finally see with a low-angle shot–a low-ceilinged space with brass chandeliers. These soldiers should project the sense of danger that we ordinarily absorb from the guards' talk in the first scene, from Francisco's uneasiness, and the others' questions about Fortinbras. But this serene space— that is, the little of it the camera allows a viewer to take in— holds no fear. The white-washed walls, the large, multi-paned windows flooding the room with sunlight, the bare, polished floors—all these have the opposite effect. . . .

FLASHES OF VISUAL PLEASURE

The only other outdoor scenes are those with Fortinbras and his army, well done in dim light with lots of trees and horses, and the graveyard scene. . . . One of these riders is Hamlet, who dismounts to talk to the captain and then speaks his soliloquy in closeup partly to the horse who shares the frame with him. . . . Though this additional touch of reality in Plummer's scene is distracting, he pulls it off by the sheer intelligence and sensitivity of his reading. Both this scene and the graveyard scene benefit from the simple outdoor setting, the first large enough to accommodate an army, the second large enough to allow for a procession far enough away from Hamlet and Horatio to realistically give them time to hide. . . . The setting unobtrusive enough to give full play to Hamlet's newly achieved serenity.

Interior space has its own problems, with settings that may clash with the play's locus. Evidently [director Philip] Saville felt that keenly, for he kept his camera tightly focused on the actors. Only a few times does the interior setting justify the location shooting—when Saville has the courage to pull away from his actors and let the setting play some part. After Horatio and Marcellus rejoin Hamlet, he runs into the castle, and they follow. Here there is a truly beautiful shot. . . . A huge arched gateway, one barred door open against the wall, the other filling half the doorframe, makes a pattern in bars of light in the gloom. The visual image may have little to do with the three men, who are dwarfed by the setting, but it is just this sort of grandeur that can give Elsinore as a location setting its potency. There is one other image in the film showing Hamlet in extreme long shot in a startling setting, heavy with light and darkness—in the midst of the "To be" soliloquy. If only Saville had had the courage to use more of these, the TV production might have been very special indeed. But to allow Hamlet's face to remain for long the size of a pea is too daring a departure from ordinary TV practice for most directors. These settings are successful because they do not have to bear the burden of atmosphere that the ghost scenes require; rather, the atmosphere is gratuitous, surprising, and correct. They are unexpected flashes of visual pleasure.

LITTLE SENSE OF THE WHOLE SETTING

All the interiors are indeed pleasing but Saville, through framing, allows us to see little of them. The squarish interior space where the king holds his council, like the hallway, is serene and empty except for a few rows of chairs, the two thrones facing the rows at some distance, a magnificent . . . tapestry before which Hamlet will first appear, and a table for Polonius and other councillors. Because of closeups we rarely get a sense of all the actors operating within a whole setting. . . . A king, especially one as genial (if cold) as this Claudius (Robert Shaw), communicates his power through his position in space. But the camera rarely affords us a view of him in his milieu [element]; instead, it frames the others separately. The queen (June Tobin) sitting on her

throne two feet or more from him appears tentative, uneasy—though young, attractive, and physically well-
endowed. Business—glances exchanged, a pat by a
courtier—tells us that Polonius (Alec Clunes) and his family
are on the rise now with this king's ascension. Laertes
(Dyson Lovell) sits in the first row of chairs facing the king,
comes into the king's space to speak and does not hesitate to
meet the king's eyes. In contrast, we see Hamlet, not part of
the group seated, only seconds before the king notices him.
Saville suggests separation: Hamlet avoids looking directly
at the king or queen; Claudius crosses the space to stand behind Hamlet briefly; before exiting, Gertrude yearns towards
Hamlet but Claudius keeps her from approaching.

When the others leave, Hamlet soliloquizes from his
mother's chair, facing the chair once his father's, now
Claudius's. Horatio, entering, indicates that Marcellus and
Bernardo do not belong in this space by holding his hand up
to stop them from following him too closely. Though Hamlet
is dark and Horatio (Michael Caine) is blond, the two standing in full-length facing profile seem an analogous pair in
the cut of their garments—knickers and doublets—differen-
tiating them from the soldiers with their gleaming armor.
This Horatio also has a pleasing sardonic way about him
that matches Hamlet's wit. Further indicating their relative
equality, after Hamlet approaches and sits in one of the
courtier's chairs, Horatio sits too, but Bernardo remains
standing while Marcellus drops for a time into a crouch. Unfortunately, we rarely see both Hamlet and Horatio on frame
at once to notice their similarities. As Horatio speaks, we see
only Hamlet's face, his sad smile, hear his sad little laugh.
All too briefly the camera gives us a four-shot for the guards'
contribution. At the end, the camera is so close to Hamlet for
his last lines that his nose is distorted.

This same space is the setting for the scene in which
Rosencrantz and Guildenstern appear and Polonius dis-
closes Ophelia's letter (2.2). Now the king is the administra-
tor, pushing papers about. Ophelia enters this room with
Polonius—obviously both are expected. Ophelia looks worried as she listens to her father and as she says a few words
from 2.1 about refusing to see Hamlet. She does not belong
in this space—the queen ignores her and the king, after a
calculating look, questions her sternly—and Polonius eases
her out before he speaks to both king and queen about spy-

ing on Hamlet. Indeed she does not seem to belong to any space. Because 2.1 is cut and no visualization is added to replace it, we never see Ophelia in a room of her own. . . .

Hamlet and Polonius each mimic the gestures of the other, with a quietly comic effect. Hamlet has not overheard Polonius plot with the king against him, does not seem to be aware that Polonius has told his daughter to deny him access to her.

A HAMLET DEEP INSIDE HIMSELF

As Polonius scurries off, frightened by Hamlet's contortions when he says "except my life," Hamlet remains in the same space for "To be, or not to be.". . .

Philip Saville has been criticized—unfairly, I think—for breaking up the words of the world's most famous soliloquy by placing it in three locations. But breaking up space is breaking up time: Saville gives us the sense of Hamlet brooding about the ideas he turns over and over in his mind in long, lonely sessions. Few Hamlets project the character's intellectuality as well as Plummer does in this sequence. No matter how close to the camera Hamlet is, his eyes never make contact with it. This is a Hamlet deep inside himself, not communicating to an audience. Except for the one beautiful extreme long shot of the medieval catacombs, a magnificent play of rough surfaced architecture, light, and shadow, Hamlet in this scene appears only in closeup or extreme closeup. Therefore, the settings and especially the changes in setting are unobtrusive yet quietly effective. Though the lobby is also where Hamlet first notices Rosencrantz and Guildenstern in the courtyard below, Saville, by moving about for "To be," does not . . . connect Hamlet to any particular space. . . . There are other ramifications as well. For one thing, we are more aware of Hamlet always alone by this fragmentation of time and space: he does not appear with Horatio or Ophelia in all his roamings through the castle, never encounters Claudius or his mother. For another, because of the essential unity of the soliloquy, he gives the impression of deeply reasoning through a problem rather than delaying revenge. He turns ideas around in his mind. "To dye, [that is] to sleepe; No more [than that].". . .

When Hamlet comes to "Thus Conscience does make Cowards of us all," the camera shows a low-angle shot of Jesus and the two thieves at Golgotha, a wall sculpture in the sixteenth-century chapel. Appropriately, Hamlet looks at Jesus as he thinks of conscience, which he says with no self-disdain. . . .

THE NUNNERY SCENE

As the last words end, the camera cuts to the wide doorway, open to the courtyard. Ophelia enters, walking past the camera, which turns to follow her, until she stops, caught in closeup, looking towards Hamlet, who is now above her in the lectern. When they begin to speak the camera shoots over his left shoulder down to her to include both of them, but as the scene proceeds, we see one or the other in closeup, mostly as each speaks, with few reaction shots. . . .

Hamlet's very lack of anger, his position above her in the pulpit, his soft, brotherly tone—he reminds one, in fact, of Laertes giving advice to his sister—suggest that his feelings for her are affectionate rather than passionate. . . .

The only flaw in the nunnery scene for me is the sudden inclusion of a large block of the setting so that we can see the shadows of Polonius and Claudius behind a magnificent window. Changes of frame size must seem inevitable, not merely motivated by the director's need to include more characters in the frame. A credible way to include them, given the style this film establishes, would have been to have Hamlet notice them, then look off frame toward the window, and then a shot showing where he is looking. Also annoying is the fact that their spying, sure to be noticed, seems impossibly inept. When he sees them and they scurry under cover, Hamlet becomes angry, but his anger is not directed towards Ophelia particularly. He descends to her, stands behind her as she sinks to a kneeling position, and continues to speak softly after a brief harangue. Since Ophelia had not heard about the plot and since the production cuts the opening lines of 3.1, we cannot implicate her in the spying. Nor does he. His tone, however, is sufficiently bitter and sarcastic to make her think him quite mad, since she has not noticed the spies. Business at the end tells us indeed that she is shocked and horrified to learn that her father and especially that Claudius have eavesdropped. Hamlet does give her head a rough push at the end to motivate her last lines, which unfortunately the young actress is not up to delivering. Her mad scene is much better, with its combination of sheer lunacy, sensuality, and slyness. . . .

CLAUDIUS, ROSENCRANTZ, AND GUILDENSTERN

Claudius's prayer scene is also set in the chapel. This time the frame is large enough to show Hamlet looking down at Claudius from above, not close enough to get to him easily. Because of the distance, we do not necessarily see this as a real opportunity. In closeup, we see the joy Hamlet feels when he says he can now kill Claudius. The joy holds as he says "and so he goes to Heaven, / And so am I reveng'd. . . ." Then, as if he has suddenly realized the import of what he has just said, his tone changes for the next lines. . . .

As Claudius rises and walks out, we become aware, perhaps for the first time, of his robe, open to reveal a bare chest, the nakedness reminding us of his sensuality. . . . Surprisingly then, Gertrude's closet has the same austere ascetic beauty as the other rooms. As usual, no establishing shot gives us a sense of the whole room; instead, the camera reveals pieces of it as they are needed. The bed is the dominant feature, and Hamlet of course flings his mother on it. There he almost wins her over with his comparison of the two kings, her locket and his, but as soon as he speaks of avoiding her husband, he loses her. The production presents the next scene as a continuation, as it should be, of the closet scene (3.4), and not as a new scene. Claudius here shows no trace of the drunkenness that had disarmed him in the play scene. He exits to find Rosencrantz and Guildenstern outside the room and sends them off, then re-enters to give and receive a fervent embrace. After Ophelia's exit from the first mad scene, the camera cuts to Gertrude's room where king and queen lie in the bed, his chest bare, she in the kind of garment that in the sixties substituted for nudity, as he engages in pillow talk. . . .

The camera had afforded glimpses of the courtyard exterior with its cobbled stones and wide expanses through many windows. From the open door leading from the courtyard Ophelia had entered the chapel. And the courtyard serves for the meeting between Rosencrantz and Guildenstern and for the entrance of the players, transposed to follow the nunnery scene. Less overpoweringly than the chapel, the courtyard can be shot in long shot to frame more than one character at a time. But the apparent inclusiveness of long shots is limited, for the camera shows Hamlet and the players in shots that exclude Rosencrantz and Guildenstern. . . .

Just as Saville kept space between Hamlet and Ophelia, so does he between Hamlet and Rosencrantz and Guildenstern; in contrast, Hamlet shares space with Horatio and the First Player. At first, Hamlet questions his former schoolfriends from a window above them. Though he had seemed happy to see them, the space tells more fully his true feelings. When he does descend to the courtyard he remains hugging the wall as they stand some feet away. He remains distant as he begins his explanation, full of self-irony and exaggerated self-pity. The camera shows no reaction shot of them but remains focused on Hamlet, who, with the words "foule and pestilent congregation of vapours," becomes serious and introspective, forgetting them until their chuckles bring him back to the present. He does not come close to them until his lines about welcome, and then his sardonic tone negates the effect of the physical closeness. After Polonius's entrance, Hamlet and his friends go into a well-practiced routine of bouncy, quick, high-stepping marches forwards and backwards, ending with Hamlet on their shoulders—all while Polonius tries to tell them about the players. The routine suggests school days together. . . .

The film departs from its usual manner for the scene between Claudius and Laertes, one of the more successful interiors in the production, but by its nature one not useful for other scenes. A high-angle shot puts the camera in the position of judge. This is the only sequence shot entirely in long shot, giving it a disorienting, distancing effect. For once we see the whole room, cell-like, very narrow, though again white-walled and sunlit. Because the production cuts Laertes's entrance before Ophelia's second mad scene, Laertes never attempts to usurp the throne and kill Claudius but rather is decidedly in Claudius's control. As the triple plot unfolds Saville shoots from an angle that shows three receding doorways, a not-too-obvious visual metaphor. . . .

PUNCTUATED BY FLAMES AND TORCHES

The space for the scene of the play-within-a-play moves from the dim corridor with gothic arches where Hamlet speaks to Horatio (but the lines on why Hamlet admires Horatio are cut) to the interior banquet room where the play is to take place. The advice to the players is cut, an opportunity some directors take to show Horatio in quiet attendance with Hamlet, implying a further relationship between the lines. . . . This Hamlet is much more alone. The main visual point Saville makes is that Hamlet gets on stage and directs the action of the mimes from there. We see the play's action in long shot, from the point of view of Claudius and Gertrude, on a dais some distance away from the stage. From reaction shots, we learn that Gertrude knows nothing about the murder, that she cares deeply about Claudius's well-being, that Horatio believes Hamlet has demonstrated Claudius's guilt. When Claudius's drunkenness puts him off his guard sufficiently to reveal something of his guilt and he exits calling for light, Saville shoots a dark adjoining hallway punctuated by flames of torches. Inside, Hamlet exultantly gnaws on a leftover bone from the banquet table.

THE PITFALLS OF THE SETTING?

In this same space, the duel ends the drama. . . . Because of the large number of courtiers and guards in the final scene, the large room can be shot from a distance without usurping the attention we must pay to the principals. Closeups, of course, reveal that Gertrude offers Hamlet the poisoned wine once she has drunk, that Laertes crosses himself as he takes the fatal rapier, that he gives Hamlet a foul blow after impatient urgings from Claudius, that the soldiers restrain Claudius after Laertes's revelation. Yet the setting allows enough space around the closeups for Laertes to make his first admission to Osric alone and for the supernumeraries [extras] to disappear while Horatio holds the dying Hamlet, the frame widening out for Fortinbras's stately entry. The film ends with the effect of his command—repeated boomings of the Elsinore cannons sound as credits appear on the screen—not with an image of Hamlet carried to the stage.

Most often Philip Saville avoids what he evidently saw as the pitfalls of the setting. But with so much restraint necessary to allow the play to play itself, is the slender margin of gain from a few apt settings—the outdoor setting for "How all occasions . . . ," the cell for Laertes's and Claudius's plot, the graveyard scene—worth the contortions necessary to reveal only enough of the other settings to convey pictures that whole settings would obscure? The actors are all remarkably comfortable in the setting, but the director's uneasiness shows in excessive closeups and poorly motivated high-angle shots. Long ago I told a friend who wanted to disguise the awkwardness of a long, narrow kitchen to pull out all the stops instead and paint stripes parallel to the long sides; rather than disguise the problem, embrace it, revel in it. He did not listen to me. Saville too, I think, should have reveled in the magnificence of Elsinore and had more faith that Shakespeare and these highly competent actors could have filled the volume. . . . What Saville needed was a more judicious blending of all kinds of shots and more courage.

A Stage Production of *Hamlet*

Richard L. Sterne

During the rehearsals for a production of *Hamlet*, the actor playing the title role invariably hones his vocal techniques and, with the help of the director, searches for the right gestures and line readings. Even actors as great as the late Richard Burton, who played Hamlet in 1964 in a widely acclaimed New York production of the play, are humbled by the experience and eagerly seek guidance. Burton was fortunate that his director was John Gielgud, perhaps the greatest and certainly the most influential Hamlet of the century. This is an excerpt from the informative and fascinating book about that legendary production by actor-composer-writer Richard Sterne, who also had a part in the show and witnessed the rehearsals. Sterne's account chronicles a private afternoon session in which Gielgud and Burton worked alone on motivation, vocal techniques, and other aspects of the performance (Sterne secretly taped the session and later obtained Gielgud's and Burton's permission to make it public). It remains a priceless and timeless record of two of the world's greatest actors teaming up in an attempt to unravel the mysteries of the world's greatest acting role.

The doors of the rehearsal hall were locked for the afternoon with Bobby the bodyguard placed on duty to allow no one to enter but Gielgud and Burton. Both men arrived at 3:00, greeted each other, and hung up their coats. Burton walked over to the platform and sat on the edge while Gielgud went over to a table and picked up his script, then sat on the end of the table. After reflecting a few seconds he began speaking:

GIELGUD   It seems to me, Richard, and I found in playing the part, that in the concern with details in each single scene one forgets the main motivation which must progress through the

Reprinted from *John Gielgud Directs Richard Burton in "Hamlet": A Journal of Rehearsals*, by Richard L. Sterne (New York: Random House, 1967), by permission of the author. Copyright © 1967 by Richard L. Sterne.

part as a whole. You said you felt this and I've felt it so often, too. But somehow you must force yourself to think of the actual action of the play. And I don't agree with Larry [Olivier], who said in the film that this is a play about a man who can't make up his mind. Surely it's about a man who cannot reconcile his own conscience with the world as he sees it, but who is able to come to this reconciliation by the end of the play. In all the play he goes through a deluded world, putting up with the persecution which one inevitably finds; and it isn't until the end of the play, after he's assembled and solidified his action, that he is able to relieve all the difficulty. And he comes back, having solved it in England.

The fight with the pirates and Hamlet's departure are in the play to show the feeling of a journey. Shakespeare does the same in *Winter's Tale* and *Tempest*. He was fascinated by journeys because they were so much more important then and took so much longer. And it has a tremendous effect on Hamlet in this play because he comes back fantastically ready to carry out his mission without complications. It's only the sight of Ophelia's body and Laertes jumping into the grave, in which Hamlet suddenly sees this young man whom he always had liked behaving exactly as *he* had done when *his* father died, in a sort of hysteria of grief. That makes him jump in and do all that violent stuff.

And immediately after he's so ashamed of his behavior, he becomes completely open and doesn't suspect any of the treachery. And Horatio, who is not a very communicative man, does suspect that there is something wrong, but doesn't seem to have the courage to deflect Hamlet from the duel because Hamlet has always been a prince and has done what he wants. Horatio is there to obey and to serve and to listen; he doesn't seem to have much closer a personal relationship. But you feel that Hamlet wants really to die, in a way, if he can kill the King in doing it, he will have accomplished his purpose. He's made a spiritual progression and feels at ease with himself. But what is so hard in the first act is to mix all the motives and keep the true line of what he's plotting to do. He obviously begins apathetically and he can't rouse himself to any action, although he hates and resents the King. Then his friends come and tell him they've seen the Ghost; something begins to happen to him, and he says he'll watch that night with them. Now the Ghost tells him about the murder, and this must be something absolutely new when he hears it. Then he's in a frenzy from the point after the Ghost disappears. All sorts of thoughts occur to him. "Shall I tell my friends?" "Should I run and kill the King?" "No. There's more to be done. I must be quite sure that it was a real spirit." And remember, you must give yourself time to put over to the audience the awful thing in your mind—which is "What shall I do next?". . .

Then in the next scene you come back and you're in a deep depression. But somehow that's wonderful musically. "To be or not to be" in the nunnery scene is like an andante after the violent rhythms of the "rogue and peasant slave" soliloquy. Like most people, Hamlet probably has a low-key reaction after all the emotion of "The play's the thing."

BURTON   Well, I think that's terribly right, you know, John. Because I know myself that one day I'm absolutely bubbling over and making jokes and being rather coarse and jumping about, and the next day I'm very down. And I think that's Hamlet's problem, too.

"MAKE A SCAFFOLD TO BUILD YOUR SPEECHES ON"

GIELGUD   Yes. First he lashes himself for his own stupidity and then he becomes despondent and feels that he doesn't care one way or another and tries to determine if everything is worth it. "Shall I kill myself and get rid of the problem?" And then he decides at the end of the speech that he *will* go on living in spite of all the drawbacks of life—the fears, the doubts, and the sufferings. He seems to doubt the Ghost a little, doesn't he? But the Ghost is a bit of a tyrant. Obviously, Hamlet was greatly in awe of him, just as Ophelia fears *her* father. But when Ophelia comes, and I think this scene is going awfully well, could we not consider it as a second development? I feel more and more that the first offstage scene when you went to her with "your doublet all unbraced" must have been an attempt to seduce her forcibly. But when you see her the second time you have another desire. You know you frightened her the last time, and I think both of you should begin it by remembering that first scene.

BURTON   I think that from the practical point, John, what we're playing at the moment is a perfect extension of "To be or not to be." It's gentle now. And particularly because I'm so rough, the more gentle I can be whenever possible, the better. Then Hamlet won't seem to be a maniac.

GIELGUD   Yes, that's true. And sometimes, Richard you're inclined to shout out very loudly on one word, rather than to build a speech to a climax of a shout on three or four lines, which to me is more effective. You keep one word high and all the rest are lost to it. And if you do this too often, it becomes dull and coarse. It's only a question of holding your own strength.

That's what is so marvelous about Edith [Evans] when she acts. She doesn't open her soul to the audience quite, except for three or four moments in the play. And in these moments she opens this window with intense feeling. It is something like a child who can hardly wait to show you something. And you lean forward and are eager to see more, and then she slams the window shut! I marvel at the way she selects the vitally telling moments. She never weeps a lot or indulges in superfluous emotion. She hits the nail on the head for every correct mood and feeling. I think you need to select your effects precisely as she does. Find the places for them and make a scaffold to build your speeches on.

BURTON   I do have a tendency, as you tell me, John, to shout. . . . The other problem that I have with speaking Shakespeare, which you know about better than anybody in the world, is speaking the verse too flatly.

GIELGUD   You just have to be careful not to jump your images, so that you don't put three images in two lines and jump on to the next image two lines away when there are other images in between. If you don't mind me telling you these things, it's simply that sometimes you go too quickly for the audience to believe you really are thinking of what you say, that's all.

AN AWFUL CLICHÉ

BURTON   Let's start and work on the "rogue and peasant slave." I'd rather not use any sort of physical violence on the "O vengeance" because they always think I'm going to smash the throne to bits or something. I did a thing in *Henry the Fifth* which got an enormous laugh, but which would not be funny in this play. In the scene where I was trying to talk French to the girl, I got very fancy and my arms went right up in the air, like this (Burton raises his arms over his head), and then I just simply dropped them. Perhaps we could do that with "O vengeance!" But stabbing the chair is so distinctive. They'd know.

GIELGUD   It is an awful cliché. It doesn't really go with this kind of production.

BURTON   That's what I think. You see, John, because of the nature of this production, there are things in this which would never work in any other.

GIELGUD   Yes, quite right.

BURTON   For instance, seeing the Ghost—which you've carefully taught me. At the back of my head I think when I play it, I'm not going to have a costume on—which I'm not. So that the simpler you make me, the better. Elizabeth's [a reference to Elizabeth Taylor, then Burton's wife] a very clever girl about such things. She said, "It was absolutely marvelous to see how John made you better, made you easier," just like that.

GIELGUD   You are very clever, too, at taking what I give you and making it your own. There are some things I think of that don't work for you, and if you did them they'd come off badly, and so you don't do them. And that's what I'm thankful for. The moment I feel that I'm giving you too much what I myself would do, then I shrink from making any comment.

BURTON   But it works for me, which is why I told you I think it was dangerous for Peter [O'Toole] to act Hamlet with Larry [Olivier] directing, because he could so obviously be tempted to mimic him. And I would be just as bad with Larry, because my build is so like Larry. We have the same kind of squatness and strength, and it wouldn't have worked.

Trying to Conceal the Soliloquy

GIELGUD   Well, let's start on this speech now. Do you think you can show more impatience in clearing the room before you start?

BURTON   Would it be too much if I made Rosencrantz and Guildenstern scurry off by sounding vicious on "Aye, so God be with you"?

GIELGUD   Good! I like that. (Burton begins with this line and then takes a pause before "now I am alone.") I think there must be more relief here. You mustn't seem tired or sad because that's all coming in "To be or not to be." Keep it energetic and perhaps follow a little where they've gone off. (Burton does twenty lines of the speech—from "O what a rogue" to "And can say nothing") I don't like it. I think it should all be quicker—your mind is so busy. The beginning was beautiful. But then it's got to come faster up to "And can say nothing." That's the first movement of the speech. Now you're taking too long with the images. If you keep them clear and make the commas right, you can go so much faster. (Burton repeats the section more rapidly.) Much better. Do you think you could put your head in your hands for "and can say nothing"? Or do you think it's too sad? (Gielgud demonstrates this action.)

BURTON   It's marvelous, John. Anything like that. What I should love to do, if you approve, is to take all the well-known passages so that the audience are not aware of them as famous speeches.

GIELGUD   Sometimes you still shout too much, like you shouted a bit too much when you said "What would *he* do"— as if you were asking somebody really there. You're alone; you needn't take it so outwardly. Then it won't seem as if you are talking to the audience. Try to conceal the fact that it's soliloquy by making it more to yourself. Don't use quite so much voice, because the moment you shout, we feel "Who's he talking to? Is somebody up there?" It's coming very well, though. . . .

The soliloquy was repeated three more times until both men felt satisfied with it. . . .

"A Sort of Glory"

BURTON   John, I think one of the things that's fascinating about the way you're directing me, where I normally went "YAH!" you've toned me down quite rightly. And this speech, which before I spoke absolutely dead quiet, we've run into— as you suggested—a rhythm. I never thought of it before as declamatory, and yet the sense says, "From this time forth, my thoughts be bloody or be nothing worth." The whole climax is that Hamlet is going forth to kill.

GIELGUD   And it's so extraordinary. You've come out of Denmark, and here you are on the plain and you're out in the air for the first time. You're away from the "confines" and "dungeons" and "prisons." And I think you come in thinking that this is glorious to see the troops going by and the snow and all that. But suddenly even this, which you thought was a wonderful change, is a terrible blow to your character because you feel that you're going off to England and escaping all that you're supposed to do. So you think "I must do something about it," and "I bloody well will, too," by the end of the speech, and "What's the matter with me?"

The death of twenty thousand men doesn't matter to you except in a grand compassionate way. It's an impersonal attitude toward it—"Five people killed in China," "fifteen in an earthquake," or "sixteen in an air crash." There is something so much more impersonal about this speech. It's away from personalities altogether. The rest of the play is a struggle between personalities—your uncle, your mother—but this is the whole world going by. And it's an example to you and a reproach to you. At the same time it's a sort of glory.

BURTON   Then I think that I should change my attitude with the Norwegian Captain. Instead of being kind, I should be indifferent.

GIELGUD   No. I think Hamlet is very interested. Suddenly you come into a new world. You've not been aware of politics or Fortinbras. This is the first time Hamlet apprehends that people are coming through the country without fighting a war. And he thinks "Where are they going to?" And "Who are they?" It's a sudden return to the interest of the world, as when you've had a private grief, or have been rehearsing a play for three weeks, and you suddenly go out and see people in the shops and you think "My goodness, this is interesting. I'd forgotten all about it."

They worked on the speech for twenty minutes. Gielgud prompted for exact readings and also played the Captain so that Burton could work into the soliloquy more easily. He suggested starting the speech with a heroic laugh, as if Hamlet were saying, "What a fool I've been."

GIELGUD   You've got to suddenly discover the army and then stop and watch it. Then it starts in a major key so that you can go back and be thoughtful during "What is a man." And when he says "Sure, He that made us," I think he recalls the same marvelous mixture of willingness to believe, combined with the terrible doubt that he had in the "What a piece of work is a man" speech. And finally it works up to a major-key climax for the end of it.

I think that's enough for today. It will be easier to apply all this when we put the drums with it tomorrow. Thank you so much, Richard.

BURTON   No. Thank you, John.

An Uncut Film Version of *Hamlet*

Richard Alleva

Shakespeare's original, uncut version of *Hamlet* runs some four hours and almost all stage and film productions of the play over the years have been at least moderately and often heavily edited. One of the chief concerns of producers, directors, and actors has been that it would be too difficult to maintain the audience's interest for so long a performance. In 1997, British actor-director Kenneth Branagh defied this logic by filming the play in its entirety. Hoping to pique audience interest and appreciation, he cast most of the roles, even the minor ones, with famous actors. Jack Lemmon played the small part of Marcellus, for example, and Robin Williams played Osric, another minor role. In this thoughtful review of the film, noted literary and film critic Richard Alleva points out the ways that doing the play uncut weakened the presentation, and also how they greatly strengthened it. In Alleva's view, Branagh's groundbreaking project was both foolhardy and magnificent, and serves as a reminder of the play's enduring flexibility and power.

Have you ever been run over by a truck and enjoyed the experience? Well . . . have you seen Kenneth Branagh's version of *Hamlet?*

Hamlet is a jungle of a play and, as he guides us through it, Branagh refuses to wield a machete. His magnificent, foolhardy movie gives us the text virtually uncut, with all its narrative detours, playful elaborations, obscure allusions, blatant and subtle jokes, topical gossip. Sometimes these elements enrich the play, but just as often they bring its main action to a temporary halt. Consider: during the hatching of

Reprinted from "A Sixteen-Wheeler: Branagh's *Hamlet*," by Richard Alleva, *Commonweal,* March 28, 1997, by permission of *Commonweal.* Copyright 1997, Commonweal Foundation.

the plot to murder his nephew, Claudius remarks that Laertes's fencing has been much praised by a Norman gallant named Lamord, and for twenty-eight dawdling lines the finer points of Lamord are discussed when all we need to know is how much Hamlet envies Laertes's skill. Derek Jacobi as Claudius treats the passage with dispatch, but it is nevertheless forty-five seconds of pure Novocaine injected directly into the viewer's brain.

There are about a score of these *longueurs* [long, dull passages] in the movie—twenty minutes of tedium. Only twenty dull minutes in a four-hour flick? But it is precisely because this *Hamlet* is four hours long that twenty minutes take a disproportionate toll on the attention span.

HAMLET ON SPEED?

Branagh was surely aware of the problem as he shot the movie; trying to prevent boredom led him into a problem with his own performance: he's turned the Dane into a bit of a speed freak. At times his fast tempos do capture the manic quality that the prince can legitimately exhibit (the "Get thee to a nunnery" passage works brilliantly at a furious clip), but occasionally they flatten nuances [subtle meanings]. Though the first half of "O what a rogue and peasant slave" plays nicely as a tantrum, the second half needs a transition into seething expectancy that the actor fails to give it. (But he hits the right note with the concluding couplet.) In the bedroom interview with Gertrude, Branagh is certainly angry enough, but he fails to register the subtler shades of desperation and loathing that this scene—surely one of Shakespeare's greatest—contains. The delivery of "How all occasions do inform against me" is a disaster, turning a scorching piece of self-shaming into a gung ho, up-and-at-'em marital tirade. Doubtless this was because Branagh placed his movie's intermission right after this soliloquy and wanted to give audiences a tingle just before their escape to the lobby. But *Hamlet* is not *Henry V* [which contains a number of rousing battle speeches].

There are other mistakes, major and minor, including a badly edited final sequence in which Fortinbras's takeover is ridiculously staged as an armed invasion. Shakespeare makes the point (properly underscored by Branagh) that Elsinore has become an armed camp against Fortinbras's approach. Branagh has ten thousand enemy soldiers charge

Elsinore castle across an open plain without benefit of Birnam Wood camouflage—and the sentries see nothing until the army gets within the walls! And why was Rufus Sewell, owner of the droopiest eyelids since Robert Mitchum's, allowed to turn the Norwegian prince into an oaf? And why was. . . .

THE VIRTUES OF WARFARE

Enough! This *Hamlet* is the most jaw-dropping film ever made from any of Shakespeare's plays. Here's why.

Of all the Bard's productions, *Hamlet* is the one that most resists the unifying hand of the director. It's not the complexity of the hero but the bursting nature of the play itself that is the problem. Where is the center in all this abundance, in this sublime variety show of the questing human spirit? But Branagh has found a center, a unifying idea that works for him and (at least while we view his movie) for us.

This theme is in the very first image: the statue of our hero's father, old King Hamlet. The monument evokes a martial ideal: warfare as an ongoing way of life and a promotion of all the virtues warfare requires—self-sacrifice, sensual restraint, physical vigor, righteous fierceness, unity of purpose. After murdering his brother, Claudius the usurper continues his brother's preparations for war against Norway, but we can see in the soft, sensual face of Derek Jacobi that Denmark has the wrong ruler if Denmark was meant to be a Viking version of Sparta [the ancient Greek city-state known for its militarism].

And, in fact, Branagh and his designers give us an Elsinore that evokes the Hapsburg dynasty in its late nineteenth-century decadence. Military uniforms are everywhere in the court but they seem to be only fashion statements—even Ophelia wears one. Young men are constantly practicing swordplay within the palace, but it is the sort of fencing employed in private duels, useless on the battlefield. Polonius is a stern *paterfamilias* [powerful father-figure] with his children but sleeps with prostitutes on the sly, and his servant Reynaldo is clearly a pimp. There are sliding doors, secret passages, and two-way mirrors in the palace: an Elsinore where courtiers must be so busy outmaneuvering each other that they have no time to strategize against the Norwegian foe. So much for self-sacrifice, sensual restraint, martial vigor, unity of purpose.

Too Much Life in the Man

And so, in this context, when the ghost summons Hamlet it's not just a call for personal vengeance but a demand that the son restore the martial integrity of the state. But, as Branagh portrays him, is the prince the right man for the job? Branagh, both as actor and director, makes us understand clearly why it is a "cursed spite" that Hamlet was born to set the times right.

I have found some fault with the star's performance but, at its best, it is a successful portrait, not of a man paralyzed by indecision or an oedipal complex, but of a mettlesome, high-pitched nature sent zig-zagging out of control by the fury coursing within him. And it's not just fury that deprives this Hamlet of his internal compass. There's too much life in the man for him to be an agent of death. When he should be detaching himself from events long enough to plan strategy, he instead savors the nuances of the moment. Using the beautiful lower range of his rather limited voice, Branagh speaks the first soliloquy, "O, that this too, too solid flesh," with a delectation of sadness that warns us that this man will never take the necessary steps to end that sadness. In the graveyard, Branagh's hushed appreciation of the passing of all earthly joy gives us a vivid look at the self-thwarting nature of the prince. A man aware that death converts all flesh, whether Caesar's or Yorick's, into dirt fit to "stop a beer barrel" might very well be a good ruler. (Frederick the Great and Winston Churchill surely had this awareness.) But any man who too keenly savors such awareness will probably never rule. Like Elsinore itself with its hectic military preparations, Branagh's Hamlet aspires to the sword in vain. The kingdom, under Claudius, is waylaid by its corruption; the prince by his sensibility.

An Effective Cast

How well Branagh understands and cinematically exploits the two-track nature of the play, the parallel unfolding of melodramatic action alongside mental frenzy and exaltation. We see the prince about to murder the praying Claudius, and he does!—a sword thrust right through the skull. But, wait, no, that was only a visual leap into Hamlet's mind. The very next shot pulls us back into reality and the prince's doubts. Let Polonius ploddingly read Hamlet's love letter to Ophelia aloud to the king and queen and we hear only a stylized piece of whimsy ("Doubt thou the stars are fire"), but when Branagh intercuts the recitation with a glimpse of Hamlet and Ophelia making love, we experience the heat of passion beneath the rhetoric.

To praise the cast justly would require another article. Suffice it to say that I found Kate Winslet frighteningly believable as the mad Ophelia burbling obscenities and endearments. Richard Briers undercuts our standard notions of Polonius by endowing the old man with shrewdness and venom. Nicholas Farrell is a burning Laertes. Derek Jacobi's Claudius is a supreme study of the connection between evil and weakness, while Julie Christie's Gertrude explores the callousness that can grow out of sexual infatuation. Michael Maloney creates the best Horatio I've ever seen: a commoner warily treading amidst aristocratic skullduggery. And, with the exception of Robin Williams's cutesy-poo Osric, all the celebrity guest-starring pays off, especially Charlton Heston's First Player, the very model of a magniloquent actor-manager, and Jack Lemmon's Marcellus, making every syllable of the "bird of dawning" speech poignantly pierce.

Underpinning all this acting and the aptly lush costuming (Alex Byrne's) and photography (Alex Thomson's) is the eclectic [musical] score of Patrick Doyle, which employs clever pastiches of Brahms (the final funeral hymn) and Bernard Herrmann (the duel) to excellent effect.

The poet Karl Shapiro once wrote that being reviewed by the critic Randall Jarrell was like being run over by a truck that didn't hurt him. After being run over by this four-hour epic, I rose quite unbruised from my seat and felt like shouting, "Run me over again, Branagh! Run me over again, Shakespeare!"

Chronology

12TH CENTURY

The *Historia Danica* (*Chronicles of the Danish Realm*), the original story of Hamlet, is written.

1532

Henry VIII breaks with the Catholic Church.

1543

Polish astronomer Nicolaus Copernicus introduces the idea of a sun- rather than earth-centered universe in his *On the Revolutions.*

1557

William Shakespeare's parents, John Shakespeare and Mary Arden, are married.

1558

Elizabeth I becomes queen of England, initiating the so-called Elizabethan age.

1559

Book of Common Prayer is made the official English liturgy.

1561

Philosopher and statesman Francis Bacon is born.

1563

Thirty-nine Articles formally state the doctrines of the Church of England.

1564

William Shakespeare is born in the village of Stratford in central England; his noted contemporary, writer Christopher Marlowe, is also born.

1566

Ovid's *Metamorphoses* are translated by Arthur Golding.

1569

John Shakespeare becomes bailiff of Stratford.

1572

Playwright Ben Jonson, who will later become a rival of Shakespeare's, is born.

1573

Architect Inigo Jones is born; poet John Donne is also born.

1574–1575

Catholics and Anabaptists are persecuted in England.

1576

London's first public theater, called the Theatre, opens.

1577

Raphael Holinshed's *Chronicles*, which will become the source for many of Shakespeare's plays, appears.

1577–1580

Englishman Sir Francis Drake sails around the world.

1582

William Shakespeare marries Anne Hathaway.

1583

Daughter Susanna is born.

1585

Twins Hamnet and Judith are born.

CA. 1586

English playwright Thomas Kyd writes *The Spanish Tragedie,* a work that popularizes the "revenge tragedy" theatrical genre that Shakespeare will later employ to write *Hamlet.*

1587

Queen Elizabeth executes her rival, Mary, Queen of Scots; at about this time Shakespeare leaves Stratford and heads for London to pursue a career in the theater.

1588

England wins a major victory over Spain by defeating the mighty Spanish Armada.

CA. 1590–1593

Shakespeare writes *Richard III; The Comedy of Errors; Henry VI, Parts 1, 2,* and *3*; and *Titus Andronicus,* his first revenge play.

1592

In Italy, the Catholic Church burns priest Giordano Bruno at the stake for advocating the idea that the stars are other suns, each having their own planets.

1593

Marlowe dies.

CA. 1593–1600

Shakespeare writes *The Taming of the Shrew; The Two Gentlemen of Verona; The Merry Wives of Windsor; Twelfth Night; Richard II; Henry IV, Parts 1* and *2; Henry V;* and *Julius Caesar.*

1594

Shakespeare joins the newly formed Lord Chamberlain's Company theatrical troupe.

CA. 1595

The Swan theater is built.

1596

Shakespeare applies for and is granted a coat of arms for his father; Hamnet Shakespeare dies.

1597

Shakespeare buys New Place, the largest home in Stratford.

1598–1599

The Globe Theatre opens; Shakespeare owns one-eighth of its profits.

CA. 1600–1601

Hamlet is written and first performed.

1601

John Shakespeare dies.

CA. 1601–1607

Shakespeare writes his great tragedies, *Othello, King Lear, Macbeth,* and *Antony and Cleopatra.*

1603

Queen Elizabeth dies; James I becomes king of England; the English conquer Ireland; the first, shortest, and most corrupt quarto of *Hamlet* appears.

1604

The Second Quarto, now called the "good quarto," of *Hamlet* is published.

1605

Repression of Catholics and Puritans in England; Gunpowder Plot to kill James I and members of Parliament; Shakespeare invests in Stratford tithes.

1607

English settlers establish the colony of Jamestown, giving England a permanent foothold in North America.

CA. **1608–1613**

Shakespeare writes *Coriolanus, The Winter's Tale, Henry VIII,* and *The Two Noble Kinsmen.*

1610

Italian scholar Galileo Galilei points his newly built telescope at the planet Jupiter and discovers four orbiting moons, proving conclusively that all heavenly bodies do not revolve around the earth.

1611

The King James version of the Bible is published.

1613

The Globe theater burns down.

1616

Shakespeare dies.

1619

The great Elizabethan actor Richard Burbage, the first person ever to play Hamlet, dies.

1623

Anne Hathaway Shakespeare dies; the First Folio, a collection of Shakespeare's complete works, is published.

1663

The renowned English actor Thomas Betterton begins performing in *Hamlet.*

1742

David Garrick, one of the greatest actors of the eighteenth century, first tackles the role of Hamlet.

1759

Lewis Hallam becomes the first important Hamlet in America.

1929

British actor John Gielgud first plays Hamlet at London's Old

Vic Theatre; his interpretation of the role becomes the most acclaimed and influential of the twentieth century.

1937

British actor Laurence Olivier, widely acknowledged as the greatest actor of the twentieth century, plays Hamlet on stage in London.

1948

Olivier releases his film version of *Hamlet,* which wins Academy Awards for best picture and actor.

1964

Gielgud directs popular actor Richard Burton in the role of Hamlet in a long-running New York production of the play; another popular actor, Christopher Plummer, plays Hamlet in a TV production shot on location at Elsinore Castle in Denmark.

1969

A film version of *Hamlet* appears starring Nicol Williamson in the title role.

1990

Popular star Mel Gibson plays Hamlet in a colorful film version directed by Franco Zeffirelli.

1997

British actor-director Kenneth Branagh releases a four-hour-long uncut film version of *Hamlet.*

FOR FURTHER RESEARCH

TEXT, ANALYSIS, AND CRITICISM OF *HAMLET*

James L. Calderwood, *To Be and Not to Be: Negation and Metadrama in* Hamlet. New York: Columbia University Press, 1983.

Paul Cantor, *Shakespeare:* Hamlet. New York: Cambridge University Press, 1989.

Maurice Charnery, *Style in* Hamlet. Princeton, NJ: Princeton University Press, 1969.

Peter Davison, Hamlet: *Text and Performance.* Atlantic Highlands, NJ: Humanities Press, 1983.

Philip Edwards, ed., *Hamlet, Prince of Denmark.* New York: Cambridge University Press, 1985.

Avi Erlich, *Hamlet's Absent Father.* Princeton, NJ: Princeton University Press, 1977.

R.A. Foakes, "*Hamlet* and the Court of Elsinore," in *Shakespeare Survey.* Allardyce Nicoll, ed., Cambridge: Cambridge University Press, 1956.

Cyrus Hoy, ed., Hamlet: *An Authoritative Test, Intellectual Backgrounds, Extracts from the Sources, Essays in Criticism.* New York: W.W. Norton, 1963.

Ernest Jones, *Hamlet and Oedipus.* New York: W.W. Norton, 1949.

Harry Levin, *The Question of Hamlet.* New York: Oxford University Press, 1959.

Mary Z. Maher, *Modern Hamlets and Their Soliloquies.* Iowa City: University of Iowa Press, 1992.

Michael Martin, ed., *Hamlet.* New York: Prestige Books, 1968.

Barbara A. Mowat and Paul Werstine, eds., *Hamlet.* New York: Simon and Schuster, 1992.

Michael Pennington, *"Hamlet": A User's Guide.* New York: Proscenium, 1996.

Marvin Rosenberg, *The Masks of Hamlet.* Newark: University of Delaware Press, 1992.

Bert O. States, *Hamlet and the Concept of Character.* Baltimore: Johns Hopkins University Press, 1992.

Rebecca West, *The Court and the Castle.* New Haven, CT: Yale University Press, 1957.

John D. Wilson, *What Happens in* Hamlet. 1935. Reprint, Cambridge: Cambridge University Press, 1964.

Louis B. Wright and Virginia A. Lamar, eds. *The Tragedy of Hamlet, Prince of Denmark.* New York: Simon and Schuster, 1958.

SHAKESPEARE'S LIFE AND TIMES

Gerald E. Bentley, *Shakespeare: A Biographical Handbook.* Westport, CT: Greenwood, 1986.

Marchette Chute, *Shakespeare of London.* New York: E.P. Dutton, 1949.

Roland M. Frye, *Shakespeare's Life and Times: A Pictorial Record.* Princeton, NJ: Princeton University Press, 1967.

François Laroque, *The Age of Shakespeare.* New York: Harry N. Abrams, 1993.

———, *Shakespeare's Festive World: Elizabethan Seasonal Entertainment and the Professional Stage.* New York: Cambridge University Press, 1991.

Peter Levi, *The Life and Times of William Shakespeare.* New York: Henry Holt, 1989.

Peter Quennell, *Shakespeare: A Biography.* Cleveland: World, 1963.

A.L. Rowse, *Shakespeare: A Biography.* New York: Harper and Row, 1963.

———, *Shakespeare the Man.* New York: Harper and Row, 1973.

SHAKESPEAREAN THEATER PRODUCTION

John C. Adams, *The Globe Playhouse: Its Design and Equipment.* Cambridge, MA: Harvard University Press, 1942.

Sally Beauman, *The Royal Shakespeare Company: A History of Ten Decades.* Oxford: Oxford University Press, 1982.

John R. Brown, *William Shakespeare: Writing for Performance.* New York: St. Martin's Press, 1996.

Cecil De Banke, *Shakespeare Production, Then and Now.* London: Hustchinson, 1954.

John Elsom, *Post-War British Theater Criticism.* London: Routledge and Kegan Paul, 1981.

Gordon Grosse, *Shakespearean Playgoing, 1890–1952.* London: Mowbray, 1953.

G.B. Harrison, *Elizabethan Plays and Players.* Ann Arbor: University of Michigan Press, 1956.

Robert Speaight, *Shakespeare on the Stage.* London: Collins, 1973.

Arthur C. Sprague, *Shakespeare and the Actor's Stage Business in His Plays (1660–1905).* Cambridge, MA: Harvard University Press, 1944.

NOTED ACTORS PORTRAY AND DISCUSS SHAKESPEARE'S CHARACTERS

Donald Brook, *A Pageant of English Actors.* New York: Macmillan, 1950.

Ivor Brown, *Shakespeare and the Actors.* New York: Coward McCann, 1970.

John Gielgud, *An Actor and His Times.* London: Sidgwick and Jackson, 1979.

Anthony Holden, *Laurence Olivier: A Biography.* New York: Atheneum, 1988.

Garry O'Connor, *Ralph Richardson: An Actor's Life.* London: Hodder and Stoughton, 1982.

Laurence Olivier, *On Acting.* New York: Simon and Schuster, 1986.

Richard L. Sterne, *John Gielgud Directs Richard Burton in Hamlet: A Journal of Rehearsals.* New York: Random House, 1967.

FILM VERSIONS OF SHAKESPEARE'S PLAYS

Richard Alleva, "A Sixteen-Wheeler: Branagh's 'Hamlet'," *Commonweal,* March 28, 1997.

Brenda Cross, ed., *The Film* Hamlet: *A Record of its Production.* London: Saturn Press, 1948. (Editor's Note: This volume is about Laurence Olivier's film version of *Hamlet,* for which he received the Academy Award for best actor.)

Charles W. Eckert, *Focus on Shakespearean Films.* Englewood Cliffs, NJ: Prentice-Hall, 1972.

Jack J. Jorgens, *Shakespeare on Film.* Bloomington: Indiana University Press, 1977.

Bernice W. Kliman, Hamlet: *Film, Television, and Audio Per-*

formance. Rutherford, NJ: Fairleigh Dickinson University Press, 1988.

Roger Manvell, *Shakespeare and the Film.* London: Debt, 1971.

Peter Whitehead and Robin Bean, *Olivier: Shakespeare.* London: Lorrimer Films, 1966.

GENERAL GUIDES TO SHAKESPEARE'S PLAYS

Isaac Asimov, *Asimov's Guide to Shakespeare.* New York: Avenel Books, 1978.

Charles Boyce, *Shakespeare: A to Z: The Essential Reference to His Plays, His Poems, His Life and Times, and More.* New York: Facts On File, 1990.

Marchette Chute, *Stories from Shakespeare.* New York: New American Library, 1956.

Norrie Epstein, *The Friendly Shakespeare: A Thoroughly Painless Guide to the Best of the Bard.* New York: Viking Penguin, 1993.

Harley Granville-Barker and G.B. Harrison, eds., *A Companion to Shakespeare Studies.* Cambridge: Cambridge University Press, 1959.

Karl J. Holzknecht, *The Backgrounds of Shakespeare's Plays.* New York: American, 1950.

Kenneth Muir and Samuel Schoenbaum, eds., *A New Companion to Shakespeare Studies.* Oxford: Oxford University Press, 1971.

The Riverside Shakespeare. Boston: Houghton and Mifflin, 1974.

GENERAL SHAKESPEAREAN ANALYSIS AND CRITICISM

Andrew C. Bradley, *Shakespearean Tragedy.* New York: Viking Penguin, 1991.

Lily B. Campbell, *Shakespeare's Tragic Heroes: Slaves of Passion.* 1930. Reprint, New York: Barnes and Noble, 1968.

Edmund K. Chambers, *William Shakespeare: A Study of Facts and Problems.* New York: Oxford University Press, 1989.

Cumberland Clark, *Shakespeare and the Supernatural.* London: Williams and Norgate, 1931.

William Empson, *Essays on Shakespeare.* New York: Cambridge University Press, 1986.

M.D. Faber, *The Design Within: Psychoanalytic Approaches to Shakespeare.* New York: Science House, 1970.

Brian Gibbons, *Shakespeare and Multiplicity.* Cambridge: Cambridge University Press, 1993.

Clifford Leech, ed., *Shakespeare: The Tragedies, A Collection of Critical Essays.* Chicago: University of Chicago Press, 1965.

Carolyn R.S. Lenz et al., eds., *The Woman's Part: Feminist Criticism of Shakespeare.* Urbana: University of Illinois Press, 1980.

Maynard Mack Jr., *Killing the King: Three Studies in Shakespeare's Tragic Structure.* New Haven, CT: Yale University Press, 1973.

Dieter Mehl, *Shakespeare's Tragedies: An Introduction.* New York: Cambridge University Press, 1986.

Clarice Swisher, ed., *Readings on the Tragedies of William Shakespeare.* San Diego: Greenhaven Press, 1996.

WORKS BY WILLIAM SHAKESPEARE

Editor's Note: Many of the dates on this list are approximate. Because manuscripts identified with the date of writing do not exist, scholars have determined the most accurate available date, either of the writing or of the first production of each play.

1 Henry VI (1591)

2 and *3 Henry VI* (1591–1592)

The Comedy of Errors; Richard III; Sonnets (1592–1593)

Titus Andronicus; The Taming of the Shrew; The Two Gentlemen of Verona; Love's Labour's Lost; publication of *Venus and Adonis* (1593)

Publication of *The Rape of Lucrece* (1594)

A Midsummer Night's Dream; Romeo and Juliet; Richard II (1594–1595)

The Merchant of Venice (1595–1596)

King John (1596)

1 Henry IV (1597)

2 Henry IV; Much Ado About Nothing (1598)

Henry V; As You Like It; Julius Caesar; The Merry Wives of Windsor; publication of "The Passionate Pilgrim" (1599)

Twelfth Night; Hamlet; Troilus and Cressida (1600–1601)

"The Phoenix and the Turtle" (1601)

Othello (1602)

All's Well That Ends Well (1603)

Measure for Measure (1604)

King Lear; Macbeth (1606)

Antony and Cleopatra; Coriolanus; Timon of Athens
(unfinished); *Pericles* (1607–1609)

Sonnets and "A Lover's Complaint" first published by
Thomas Thorpe (1609)

Cymbeline (1610)

The Winter's Tale (1610–1611)

The Tempest (1611)

Henry VIII (1612–1613)

INDEX